DATE DUE			

Cat Breeding
and
Showing

Cat Breeding
and
Showing
A Guide for the Novice

Meredith D. Wilson

South Brunswick and New York: A S. Barnes and Company
London: Thomas Yoseloff Ltd

© 1972 by A. S. Barnes and Co., Inc.

A. S. Barnes and Co., Inc.
Cranbury, New Jersey 08512

Thomas Yoseloff Ltd
108 New Bond Street
London W1Y OQX, England

Library of Congress Cataloging in Publication Data

Wilson, Meredith D.
   Cat breeding and showing.

   1. Cats.   I. Title.
SF447.W76   636.8'082   74-37821
ISBN 0-498-01074-0

Printed in the United States of America

To my daughter,
Dawn,
and
in loving memory
of
her great-grandmother.

Contents

Acknowledgments

My sincere thanks to those who have helped make this book possible. Thank you to those who sent invaluable information and to those who gave willingly of their pictures. Last, but certainly not least, a thank you to my own cats who helped by not trying to help too much.

Sandra Middleton
Siamese Cat Society of America, Inc.
Mrs. J. W. Dickson, Namekagon Cattery
Liesa F. Grant
Mrs. W. Daly, Cats of Dalai
Rindy's Haven, Mr. Ed. Rindfleisch
American Cat Association
American Cat Fanciers Association
Cat Fanciers Association
UCF
UCFA
Cat Fanciers Federation
Mrs. Barbara Barrett, Wah-Bash Cattery
Mrs. Jane Martinke
Mr. Robert Lane
Mrs. Marian Newton
Miss Sonya Stanislow
Mrs. Loretta Ruzinsky
Mr. and Mrs. Tracey
Mrs. James Estes
Mr. William Bryan
Mrs. Mary Leibold

Mr. Wain Harding
Alda Zanetti
Pet Pride

Cat Breeding
and
Showing

1
Breeds: To Each His Own

THE ABYSSINIAN

This cat has been considered the Sacred Cat of Egypt and the Wild North African Desert Cat. Shorthaired and first brought into England in the 1800s by an officer in the Abyssinian War from Africa, it is affectionate, graceful, and alert. In addition it is known for being playful, loving its freedom, being active; and for its slender, beautiful body. Its head is slightly round and wedge-shaped. It has a wide forehead with a slight rise from the bridge of the nose to the forehead. The muzzle is not too pointed. The Abyssinian is long and lean with a fine bone structure and a body that seems to flow. It loves to use its paws to play with and hold objects. It is also the most susceptible to disease among the breeds. The body is medium long, not too large, graceful, and well developed. The head is smaller than the Siamese. The ears are not so large, but are alert looking and still pointed. The inside of the ears is bare and open. The cat has a fairly long tail, thick at the base, but tapering to the tip. The legs are slim, fine-boned and end in small, neat feet.

The *Ruddy color* has black or brown ticking on the hair (two or three bands of color on each hair). There is a dark spine line and the belly tint harmonizes with the main color, an orange-brown shade. The coat is short, fine, and close. The pads are black and extend up the back of the hind legs. The eyes are large, almond-shaped, bright, and expressive;

13

Ruddy Abyssinian
Gr. and Quad. Ch. Bili Basha's Rebekka
Sire: Tr. Ch. Bili Basha's Balsam
Dam: Bili Basha's Naomi
Owner: Mrs. Albert W. Dickens
Photo: Thelma Cohen

they may be green, gold, or hazel.

The *Red variety* is a rich copper. Ticking is darker. The underside (belly and hind legs) is dark brown and may continue as a dark line up the tail. The dark brown coloring around the pads, which extends up the back of the hind legs, is characteristic. Pads and nose are pink; eyes are gold or hazel.

FAULTS: bars, rings or tabby markings; necklaces, white on body, belly spots, grey color tones, cobby build, round head, extreme wedge, long angular wedge, small ears, pale, small eyes; coarse, thin or long coat.

THE AMERICAN DOMESTIC SHORTHAIR

This cat is known in Continental Europe as the European shorthair and in England as the British shorthair. It is believed to have come to America in the 19th century with English, Spanish, Dutch, and Portuguese immigrants. Its origin may date back to the British wildcats that existed after the Roman Conquest of Britain in the last century B.C. It was adopted as a breed by CFA in 1956. It is most commonly known as the "common cat." This is a fallacy. People do not generally own cats just like these. Domestic shorthairs are bred for specific features, and can trace their ancestry as far back as can any pedigreed cat.

It is the hardiest of the breed. Its face is broad and the cheeks developed, especially in the male stud (in all breeds you will find that the males will develop a more pronounced jowl each time they breed). The nose and face length is medium short. The eyes are round, set far apart. The muzzle is squarish. The ears are wide set and medium in size with rounded tips and not large at the base. The neck is medium short and is strong looking. The chin should be perpendicular with the upper lip. The animal is well developed, large but not awkward. The far set eyes show off the broad nose. Eye color will correspond to the coat color.

Red tabby American Domestic Shorthair
Gr. Ch. and Tri. Ch. Solon Red Afterglow
Sire: Tri. Gr. Ch. Solon Red Embure
Dam: Solon Blue Mist
Owner: Mrs. Ernest A. Miller

Brown male tabby American Domestic Shorthair
Gr. Ch. Male Man of DeTracey
Owner: T. W. Tucker

Female tortoiseshell American Domestic Shorthair
Gr. Ch. Rococo Ruby Begonia
Sire: Gr. Ch. RichMar's Eric the Red of Rococo
Dam: Gr. Ch. Esquire Sapphire of Rococo
Breeder/Owner: Mr. Jim Shinkle

These cats are medium to large in size. They have short, muscular legs, full chests, and deep bodies. The feet are rounded. The tail is in proportion to the body: thick at the base, but tapering to a point at the end and carried level with the back. It is fairly thick. The coat is short, close lying, thick and even in texture. It should be shining. The cat is muscular but graceful, powerful but well knit.

FAULTS: fat or skinny, kinks, white spots, fine, thin coat; long, fluffy textured coat; long nose, wedge-shaped head, long pointed ears, neck too short and thick; neck too long or slender; weak receding chin, narrow slanting eyes, too stocky or oriental sleekness.

THE ANGORA (ANKARA)

This cat comes directly from a province in Turkey known both for its Ankara goat and for its cat. (The goat is known for its long silky hair and provides mohair. At first they came to this country, into New England, from the Orient.) Through inbreeding with the Persian the cat became extinct in the United States in the 1900s. In Ankara, Turkey, they are prized and kept in zoos. The first pair to be brought here in recent years arrived in 1962, imported by Walter and Liesa Grant. In 1966 another unrelated pair was bought by the same couple and breeding is carefully taking place.

Though they used to come in many colors—including smoke, black, light and dark beige—now only the white remains, with the odd eyed being the most desired. Another factor is that deafness is common to these cats. Their heads are wedge-shaped, small in the female and medium in the male. The skull is wide at the top and gently tapers. The eyes are round, the nose medium long and curved, but with no break. The chin is rounded and the jaw tapered. The neck is slim and graceful. The chest is light framed, with the rump slightly higher than the front of the cat. The body is long and graceful. The ears are wide set, wide at the base and pointed with tufts. They have a long, full, bushy tail, wide at the base, tapering to narrow at the end. The tail is carried horizontally over the body and almost touches the head. The fur is longer at the ruff than the body coat and is silky with a wavy tendency. The paws are small and round and the pads are pink as is the nose leather. The colors are white, with copper, blue and odd eyes. They are responsive, intelligent, alert, not talkative, adaptable, loyal, and learn quickly. They are normally healthy and hardy. They are available from Turkey with a bill of sale, certificate of ancestry, short records and import-export papers.

FAULTS: any color other than white, Persian body type, cobby.

Amber-eyed female ankara and odd eyed kitten ankara
Yildizcek and Talinli
Owner: Liesa and Walter Grant

THE BALINESE

The Balinese has a long history since it developed from a mutation into a separate breed. The Balinese came into being first when at Rai-Mar Cattery Mrs. Marion Dorsey found white fuzzy kittens among her purebred Siamese litter. Mrs. Helen Smith of Merry Mews around the same time had a similar occurrence. The breeders accepted them as a new breed—longhaired Siamese. Mrs. Sylvia Holland of Holland Farm Cattery bought one such cat and so did Mrs. Mildred Alexander. Donald and Elaine Young of Ti-Mau Cattery bought several as did Kirsten Hovde of

Balinese seal point male
Dbl. Ch. and Ch. E.L.C. Kats Douzie Touzie of Wah-Bash
Breeder: Mrs. E. F. Crouch
Owner: Mrs. Barbara Barrett

Balinese kittens: sealpoint and blue point males
Breeder/Owner: Mrs. Barbara Barrett

Chen Ye Cattery. Ruby M. Green's Verde Cattery developed a new bloodline and combined it with Holland Farm's. Many other breeders joined the ranks, breeding for these cats and bettering them along the way. Mrs. Helen Smith was not happy with the name Longhaired Siamese and thought they had the grace and beauty of a Balinese dancer and thus the name. They were recognized in 1963 by CFF.

This cat's face is long, tapering, and medium wedge-shaped. The wedge starts at the nose and breaks out to the tips of the ears forming a triangle. The width of the eyes is the distance between the eyes. The skull is flat. There is no break at all, no dip in the nose and no bulge over the eyes. The nose is long and straight. The chin is medium in size. The tip of nose and chin should line up vertically. The ears are rather large, pointed, alert, wide at the base and perked forward. The eyes are almond, but more round than the Siamese. They are medium in size, slant toward the nose, and are not crossed. It has a graceful, muscular, sleek and long body, with fine bones and firm muscles. The hips are never wider than the shoulders. The abdomen is tight as are the lower ribs. The neck is long and slender. The legs are long and slim, with hind legs longer than the front. The paws are small and oval. The tail is plumelike, long, thin, the fur lies naturally, and the tail tapers to the point with no kink. The coat is long, fine, silky, and flowing toward the rear. There is a medium neck ruff. The hair is around the ankles, but not on the feet. All points should be the same shade. The mask is connected to the ears by tracings. It does not extend over the head. No white or color bands should appear in the points. Light body hairs tend to fall over the legs in a soft and silky manner. The color is the same as the Siamese but may be a little darker. It comes in Bluepoint, Chocolate point, Frost point, and Seal Point. The eyes are blue, a deep clear blue.

FAULTS: body spots, weak hind legs, a kink, similarity to the Persian, eye color other than blue, white toes or feet.

THE BIRMAN

The Birman or Burman is an exotic and lovely cat, also known as the Sacred Cat of Burma. Hundreds of these cats are believed to have lived in underground temples in Burma. The Kittah priests believed the faithful returned to earth in the bodies of these cats, which was the reason why they were worshipped. Then they went to Tibet and on to Cambodia. It was here that a Mr. Townes in 1959 brought a pair from the sacred Temple of Lao-Tsun. In this country a Mrs. Griswold took up the job and pleasure of breeding these cats.

They are known to be loving, affectionate, smart, and possessed of a sweet voice. Their heads are broad, strong, and rounded. There is a round flat spot in front of the ears. The forehead slants backward. The nose is a medium one, on which the nostrils are set low. The cheeks are full and the jaw is heavy. The chin is fully developed, and if the cat is in proportion, it is in line perpendicularly with the upper lip. All in all the face is round and has the look of strength and fullness. The ears are medium in length and width. The eyes are almond and round. The body itself is long and of medium length. Its lovely coat is long and silken, and the ruff around the neck is very heavy. Sometimes there is curly hair on the stomach. The cat is colored like the Siamese, with color points on the mask, ears, legs, and tail. The cat has the blue eyes of the Siamese also. However, the front paws are white across the third joint and the back paws are entirely white with the white continuing up the back of the legs. In all they are well proportioned, unique, and beautiful.

Standard Colors
BLUE POINT: The body is bluish white, cold in tone, shading gradually to an almost pure white on the stomach and chest. Points are deep blue except for the white gloves. The

Sealpoint female Birman
Ch. Janacques Parvula of Skybrook
Sire: Fairos de Lugh (Imp.)
Dam: Janacques Deesse
Breeder: Dr. John H. Seipel
Owner: Sheryl Van Gundy

nose is slate, the pads are pink. The eyes are blue, the more violet the better.

CHOCOLATE POINT: The body is ivory with no shading. Points except white gloves are milk-chocolate-warm in tone. The nose leather is cinnamon pink and the paw pads are pink. The eyes are a violet blue.

LILAC POINT: The body is glacial tone verging on white with no shading. Points, except the gloves, are frosty grey with pinkish tone. Nose leather is lavender pink and the pads are pink. The eyes are blue-violet.

Sealpoint Birman
Praha-Hu-Tsung
Owner: Elsie Fisher

SEAL POINT: The body is an even pale fawn to cream, warm in tone, shading gradually to a light color on the stomach and chest. Points, except gloves, are deep seal brown. Gloves are pure white. Nose leather is the same as points. The paw pads are pink. The eyes are blue, the more violet the better.

FAULTS: Lack of white glove on any foot, areas of pure white anywhere else, kink, crossed eyes, Siamese type head.

THE BRITISH BLUE

The head of this cat is broad with well rounded contours. The nose is short and broad. There is a fair shaped muzzle. Large round eyes are set wide apart. The ear set is important. They are medium in size and set far enough apart so that the base of the inner ear would be perpendicular to

the outer corner of the eye. The ears are broad at the base
and rounded at the tips. The neck is short and bull-like,
particularly in the male. The eye opening is round and set to
show the breadth of the nose. The color of the eyes is
copper or amber, the more copper the better. The eyes are
medium to large in size. The shoulders are broad and flat.
Hips are the same width as the shoulders. The chest is
broad and rounded. The cat is well knit and powerful. The
legs are short and heavy boned. The feet are well rounded
as are the toes. The tail is in proportion to the body. It is
thick at the base with a slight taper. The color is light to
medium blue. There should be no shadings or marking or
white. The coat is short, well bodied and firm to the touch.
It is not double, or open. Blues are gentle cats and easy
to handle.

THE BURMESE

Selective breeding for this lovely animal was begun in
1930 by C. Thompson with a sealpoint Siamese male hybrid
named Wong Mau. They are similar to the Siamese, of
medium size, heavier than they look and very lovable, with
beautiful coats and a rich solid color. It has good bone
structure and muscular development. Its face is round, its
head big and round, with width between the ears. The face
has a sweet expression and expressive, huge eyes. The face
tapers to a short but well developed muzzle. The nose
break is visible. The neck is short, thick, and muscular. The
cat's medium-sized ears are set apart, tilted slightly forward, broad at the base and slightly rounded at the tip.
The legs are short, the front ones wide set, giving the
chest a large, rounded appearance. The eyes are round and
set apart, yellow to gold in color. The body is medium in
size and muscular; the back is level and the general appearance is roundish or cobby. Its rump is well rounded and its
medium-sized paws are round. The tail is straight, with a

Sable Burmese
Int. Ch. Rangoon's Candy of Sher-Ming
Sire: Gr. Ch. Kittrik's Gung-Ho of Silkwood
Dam: Ch. Senshu's Toffee of Rangoon
Owner: Theresa C. Seward

blunt rounded end, carried lower than level of the back and of medium length. Its coat is fine, glossy and satin-like, short and close lying.

They Come in Four Colors

BLUE: Bright silvery grey with warm overtones. Nose leather is dark blue grey with foot pads a flesh blue grey.

CHAMPAGNE: Warm beige shading to pale gold. Tan underside. Pads and nose leather are light brown. There may be shading on face and ears.

SABLE: Brown, warm rich sable. Underparts lighter. Pads and nose leather is brown.

PLATINUM: Light bright silvery platinum grey with overtones of pinkish grey. Nose leather greyish pink. Pads are pink.

FAULTS: green or blue eyes, white spots, kinked tail, white whiskers.

THE EGYPTIAN MAU

The Egyptian Mau is the descendant of the sacred cat of Egypt and therefore one of the oldest of the cat breeds. The only natural breed of spotted cat, they first appeared in history in the art work of the ancient Egyptians, who considered it a god. They represented the light born of darkness and were greatly worshipped. These cats had two types of markings. Some had the lined markings of the striped tabby; others were spotted. In appearance they had long legs and a long tail, a narrow chest and long body. The shoulder blades are prominent.

Today's Egyptian Mau (they were first brought to the United States in 1953) is spotted randomly. The legs are banded. In the coat is a pattern somewhere between spots and stripes. The spots vary in shape and size. There are two recognized colors: Silver and Bronze. The Silvers have a lighter silver ground color with black markings. The Bronzes have a ground color lighter than that of the Abyssinian and with dark brown markings. A good specimen of the breed has at least one broken necklace under the chin. There is also a stripe that runs the length of the body to the tip of the tail on the back. The eyes are gooseberry green, but may change to amber and back without warning.

Bast's Ici Bronze Female Egyptian Mau
Breeder/Owner: Wain Harding
Photo: Robert Chorneau

They are friendly, shy and have a quiet voice. They are active and move easily. The male is always much larger than the female.

Bast's Gieda
Breeder/Owner: Wain Harding
Photo: Robert Chorneau

THE EXOTIC SHORTHAIR

This is a shorthair cat with Persian body type. It also comes in the same variety of Persian colors. First recognized as different from the American domestic and, thanks to Mr. Robert Lane, President of the Exotic Shorthair Fanciers and Jane S. Martinke, it gained acceptance as a breed. A hybrid, it is the result of a Persian introduced into an American Domestic Shorthair. Its head is round and massive. The skull is broad and the face is round. The neck is short and thick. It has a short, flat, and broad nose. Its cheeks are full and jaws and chin are powerful and broad. Its shoulders too are broad. The ears are small, round tipped, tilted forward, not too open at the base. They are set far apart and low on the head, fitted to the roundness of the head. The eyes are large, round, and full. They are set wide and are bright and sweet. The body is cobby, low on its legs, with a deep chest, broad shoulders and rump. It has a short, well-developed midsection with a level back. The forelegs are straight. The tail is short and carried without a curve and at an angle lower than the back. The coat is medium length and a soft texture. Signs of cross breeding are flowing fur, blue-green or copper eyes, legs too short, or a space between shoulders and hips.

THE HAVANA BROWN

This cat was developed by a planned breeding program. It originated in England in the 1950s with the color of the "Swiss Mountain Cat." It came to the United States in 1956 after being recognized in England. It is also known as Chestnut Brown. Two breeding programs were carried out in this country. The first was by Mrs. Hargraves and Mrs. Von Uilman who crossed a chocolate point Siamese and a black domestic. In the second breeding program a sealpoint Siamese was crossed with a Russian blue. Finally in 1960 the breed Havana Brown was recognized by the American associations.

It is a cat somewhere between the shorthair American Domestic and the Siamese. It is intelligent, playful, learns tricks easily, loves people. The kittens look like bear cubs. The cats are a bronzy-red brown to a solid darker brown, the color of ripe chestnut. They are graceful and royal.

Speedy Gonzales of the Katerwol
Breeder: Mary DePew
Owner: Mr. and Mrs. Charles L. Schmidt

New lines are now being developed by such people as Mrs. John Dickson of NameKagon Cattery. The head of this cat is longer than wide with a good break at the eyes. The head narrows to rounded muzzle with a break behind the whiskers. The whiskers are brown. The ears are large and round tipped, with little hair inside or outside the ear. They are wide set with no flair. The body is medium length, medium heavy, and thick, not cobby and not slinky. The cat is firm and muscular. The neck is also medium length, firm, and muscular. The legs are long and slim, ending in oval

Namekagon Brown Legend, Quad. CH.
Breeder/Owner: John and Velta Dickson

paws. The wide tail is medium in length, not short or thick, or long like the Siamese. The coat is medium in length and smooth. The color is rich, warm mahogany brown, all the same shade to the skin, but the under shade may be lighter. The nose and pads are a rosy brown tone. The coat is soft, silky, open, and glossy. The eyes—expressive, oval, brilliant —are a chartreuse or dark green. The voice is a soft cry.

FAULTS: white whiskers, weak chin, black nose and paw pads, Siamese head, no break, kink.

THE HIMALAYAN

The Himalayan or "Colourpoint," as it is known in England, originated as a cross between a Persian and a Siamese, but now stands as a breed by itself. No longer do people breed Himalayans by matching Persian to Siamese, but instead breed Himalayan to Himalayan in an effort to improve an already beautiful and unique breed. It was originated in this country by Marguerita Goforth and in England by Brian Sterling-Webb of Briarry Cattery. Both had the same idea at approximately the same time. Longhaired Siamese (mutations) had been appearing in litters as early as the mid-1930s, and finally in 1937 a longhaired Siamese was actually shown in Boston. In 1957 the Himalayan was finally recognized as a breed, and since then it has been getting increasingly more popular. Mrs. Goforth, when she began in 1950, was breeding for the Persian body type, or "cobby" type as it is called, with the Siamese color points and deep, blue eyes. She took the name from a rabbit called the Himalayan, which has the same color point markings. When she left off, Jean Sugden of Sugden Cattery and the Borretts of Chestermere Cattery took over.

The Himalayan should have color points similar to the Siamese and deep, blue eyes, the deeper the better. Its head should be large and round. The width between the ears should be wide (the breadth of the skull) and the neck should not be too long, but be strong and short as in the Persian. The cheeks should be full and well developed. The cat should have a well-developed chin and a powerful jaw. The ears are small, tilted forward and rounded at the tip, but not too open at the base. The eartufts should be long. The eyes are large, round, wide set and the face above all should have the Persian's sweet expression. The nose is small, with a definite break—where the nose stops abruptly at the forehead. The fur is long and the cat characteristically had a full ruff and a frill between the front legs.

Bluepoint male kitten
Pearl Harbor Tiftan of Lyford
Sire: Pearl Harbor Cheeko
Dam: Pearl Harbor Cindy
Owner: Terry and Harold Brule
Best Himalayan kitten five times

Its body should be short and "cobby" with a deep chest and width across the shoulders and rump. The back is straight, level, and firm; and the midsection is rounded and also firm. The legs are short, thick, and strong. The forelegs should be straight. Its tail should be fluffy and short and be carried lower than the back without dragging and without a curve.

Sealpoint female kitten
Zig-Lee's Nanny Tanny of Theta
Sire: Gr. Ch. Chi Chi of Himba-tab
Dam: Harobed's Monique of Zig-Lee
Owner: Merry and Bob Wilson
Breeder: Mrs. Donald Zigray

The cat's disposition is a cross between its ancestors. It is sweet, docile, beautiful, affectionate, but intelligent and playful with a voice more subdued than the Siamese but louder than a Persian. They are born white, usually, with the color points developing later.

FAULTS: a narrow chest and large pointed ears; a long tail, long nose, long legs; a Siamese head that is thin with a long muzzle and narrow head; a long back, thin legs, a thin neck, small oval feet, separated toes, a long, tapering, kinked tail; close short fur, tabby markings, spots on the belly, shadings that are off color, and uneven body color.

The Himalayan has color points similar to the Siamese; namely, Chocolate Point, Lilac Point, Seal Point, Flame or Red Point, Blue Point, Blue Cream Point, Lynx Point and the Torti Point. There is no Albino Point.

Sealpoint male
Quad. Ch. Sugden's KO-KE of Regal (Imperial) Crown
Sire: Briarry Jasper of Sugden (Imp.)
Dam: Sugden's Sanchita
Owner: Loretta Ruzinsky
Photographer: Robert Salvato

Sanga's Snow Sparkle of Theta
Lilac Point Himalayan Male
Sire: Mink Queen Astredo of Kenlyn
Dam: Kenlyn's Impomia Hapi Nu-Nu
Breeder: Garnet and Sandra Middleton
Owner: Merry and Bob Wilson

Flame Point Male
Quad. Ch. Raylyn's Taurus of Devine
Sire: Ch. Chesterhill's Tabasco of Raylyn
Dam: Ch. Raylyn's Carousel
Owner: Peter and Brenda Devine

THE KORAT

This cat gets its name from the Siamese *Si-Sawat*, which means cat color of seed of wild fruit (*Si*) and good luck (*Sawat*). The cat comes from Thailand's Korat Plateau, in the northeastern province of the same name. They are

Korat female
Dbl. Ch. Jest-O's Su-Zee
Sire: Si-Sawat's Mongleur
Dam: Gr. Ch. Rosan's Sumalee
Breeder: Jack and Estelle Ours
Owner: Marion L. Newton

believed by the people of Thailand to be "good luck" cats. They move gently, softly and cautiously. They are sweet and even-tempered and do not talk much. Their heads are heart-shaped. There is a wedge between the eyes. The cat has a well-developed muzzle. The forehead is large and flat. There is an indentation in the male in the center of the forehead which accentuates the heart-shaped appearance of the face. It has a strong chin and jaw. There is a slight break, and a short nose with a downward curve. The ears are large and round tipped. There is a large flare at the base, set high on the head, with an alert look. The insides of the ears have no tufts. The eyes are large and shiny, prominent, wide and open, and oversized for the face. The eye opening has a slant when the eye is closed. The eyes themselves are a brilliant amber green. Kittens have blue eyes first, then yellow or amber color. The cat is medium in size, semi-cobby body and muscular. They are of medium bone structure. The back is curved. The legs are medium with oval feet. The tail is medium long, heavier at the base, tapering to a rounded tip. The coat is single layered, short, glossy, fine, soft, and lies close to the body. It is blue all over, tipped with silver without shadings or markings. The sheen shows where the coat is short. Paw pads are dark blue ranging to lavender with pinkish tinge. The nose leather is dark blue or lavender.

FAULTS: kink or incorrect number of toes.

THE LAVENDER FOREIGN SHORTHAIR

The head is moderately wedge-shaped, medium long, and well-proportioned. It tapers to a fine muzzle. There is no break, but it is straight from the center of the forehead to the tip of the nose and from the tip of the nose to the chin. Jowls in the stud cat are common. Ears are erect, large, wide at the base and perked.

The cats are, as a breed, medium in size, a little heavier

American Lavender Shorthair male
Tri. Ch. Chinchelita Mr. Swinger
Sire: Glory-S Banjo of Chinchelita
Dam: Orphan Annie of Chinchelita
Owner: Elita Cooper
Photo: Classic Custom Candids

boned than the Siamese, sturdier in type. They are long, graceful, firmly muscled. Overall they are elegant and robust. The neck is in proportion to the size of the body. The legs and feet are in proportion, with hind legs slightly higher than the front. The paws are oval. The tail is long and gracefully tapered; it is proportioned to the body. The eyes are almond and in color a medium to deep green. The coat is short and fine, glossy and close lying. The color is mauve or lavender on the body, with a silvery lavender cast at the roots and insides of legs. A ring of silver goes around the feet and muzzle. The nose and pads are a rosy tone as are the inside of the ears.

FAULTS: a round head, broad muzzle, small or short ears, too closely set ears, short, thick tail, kinked tail, round or crossed eyes, tabby marking, or blue or black on nose or pads.

MAINE COON CAT

This cat is a semi-longhair lacking the thickness of the longhair but with much longer hair than the shorthair. They are alert, rugged, and love the cold weather. They are believed to be a combination of a tabby and Persians brought to Maine by seamen from Europe.

Their heads are medium wide, with wide eyes that are wide set. The eye color can be green-gold or green, or any color that conforms to the coat color. Allowance is made for underdeveloped eye color in kittens. The cheek bones are high. The nose and face are medium long and the muzzle is squarish. The chin is firm and in line with the upper lip and nose. There is no break. The ears are large and wide with ear tufts circling behind the ears. The ears taper to a round point and are wide set and wide at the base. The eyes are round, large, alert. The chest is full and from medium to large. The tail is long, as is the whole

Parti-color brown tabby with white male Maine Coon
Gr. & Int. and Quint. Ch. & RM Tr. Ch. Dauphin de France
of Tati-Tan
Sire: Kris Kringle
Dam: Petite Bon-Bon
Owner: Sonya Stanislow

cat. It is full at the base and tapers to an abrupt end. The
legs are of medium, well-proportioned height. The back is
level. The feet are large, well-tufted and round with five
toes in front and four in back. The fur on the shoulders is
short, heavier toward the end of the cat; it is almost bushy
at the end. The hairs on the sides get longer as they reach

Brown tabby male Maine Coon
Tr. Ch. RM Dbl. Ch. Tati-Tan's Beau de France
Sire: Int. and Quad. Ch. Dauphin de France of Tati-Tan
Dam: Ch. Tatiana of Tati-Tan
Breeder/Owner: Sonya Stanislow

Red tabby male Maine Coon
Int. and Quad. Ch. Tati-Tan's Bijou
Sire: Int. and Quad. Ch. Dauphin de France of Tati-Tan
Dam: Tatiana of Tati-Tan
Breeder/Owner: Sonya Stanislow

Blue male Maine Coon
Tri. Ch. Senator Muskie of Norwynde
Owner: Lillias and Joseph Vanderhoff

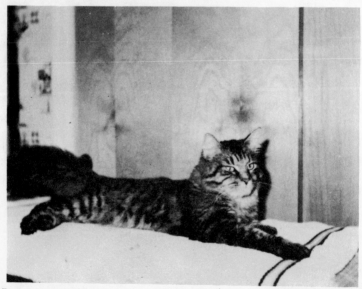

Brown mackerel tabby male Maine Coon
Tri. Ch. Norwynde Mingo
Owner: Lillias and Joseph Vanderhoff

Female blue-cream mackerel tabby with white Maine Coon
Tri. Ch. Norwynde's Mindi-Blu
Owner: Lillias and Joseph Vanderhoff

the stomach. The texture is fine and heavy. There can be a white trim around the lips, chin, muzzle; faint tabby markings and an undeveloped coat is allowed in kittens.

FAULTS: short flat face, long pointed nose, short tail, small ears, cobby body, short neck, oriental look, short legs, untufted feet, even coat length, wedge-shaped head; short, rounded, narrow-set ears; slanted eyes.

The colors that are common are similar to those of the Persian.

THE MANX

These are the tailless cats from the Isle of Man. Many stories revolve around these cats. One claims that they lost their tails when they were the last to board the ark, and had their tails cut off by the closing door. Other people believe that they first came from their homeland by way of ships wrecked on our shores. They still do reside, however, on the Isle of Man, in the center of the Irish Sea. They have come to be known as the "rumpy cat."

Many breeders still go directly to the Isle of Man to continue breeding these cats in this country, where they first appeared in New Jersey in 1820. Mr. William T. Bryan of Mt. Snaefell Cattery is one who is perfecting this breed. He says: "Our Manx are bred from 100 percent import lines of pure bred Manx selected by us on periodic trips to the Isle of Man. . . . Breeding programs go on with offspring from our imports. We are dedicated to ethical breeding of the Manx . . . by breeding true Island Manx to true Island Manx . . . to produce better colors, coats, physical lines and dispositions. We will not experiment with other breeds by mating them to our Manx for any reason. The Manx of Mt. Snaefell are always named after Kings or Queens of the Manx people from many centuries ago, or from important things pertaining to the Island. Mt. Snaefell Cattery gets its name from Mt. Snaefell, the highest peak on the Isle of Man."

These cats are completely tailless. At the end of their spine is a hollow. Their rump is rounded and they have a short, arched back. A slight rise may be seen at the end of the spinal column, but it is not considered part of a tail unless it is movable. The hind legs should be longer than the front legs and the rump higher. The cat rests on these hind legs. The flanks should be deep. The cat has a hopping gait like a rabbit because of its build. The cat should be sturdy, stout, but not fat. It should have a deep chest, with

Black male Manx
Gr. Ch. Glendower's Bruce
Sire: Ch. Tyoh Ballawilleykilleg
Dam: Gr. Ch. Ramayan Daisy Mae
Breeder/Owner: Mrs. Margaret Thompson

front legs set apart with a sturdy structure. The head is round and large, slightly longer than broad. The cheeks are prominent. Jowls are. apparent. The nose is straight, the

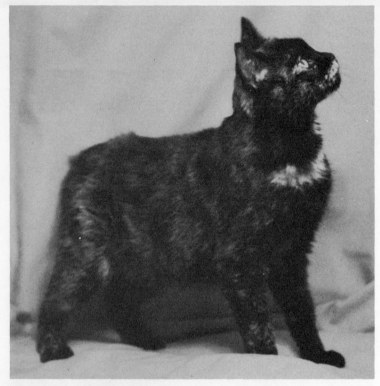

Tortoiseshell female Manx
Gr. Ch. Tra-Mar's Nutmeg
Breeder: Mrs. Marion Hall
Owner: Mrs. Franklin A. Bolin
Photo: Mr. Wayne Catto

ears medium in size, wide at the base, and tapering slightly to a point. The eyes are large, round, and wide with the outer corner a little above the inner corner. The coat should appear a double thickness, soft and open. The undercoat is thick and soft. The cat is known for its affectionate nature, alertness and bravery, as well as for its playful, healthy, and robust nature. In pose, the cat appears with its back arched, hind legs stretched, head lowered, and rump up. All colors of the Persian are typical to the Manx also.

FAULTS: a movable tail, overweightness, eyes that are straight set, a level back, extra toes, short hind legs, fine bones, knock-kneed hind legs, and a prominent rise of the bone at the end of the spine.

THE OCICAT

This cat first appeared as an accident in a litter produced

Dalai Kitty Hawk
Sire: Quad. Ch. Whitehead Elegante Sun
Dam: Dalai She
Breeder/Owner: Mrs. Virginia Daly

by a chocolate point Siamese, "Sunny," and an Abyssinian-
Siamese hybrid, "She," at Cats of Dalai. It was first thought
to be a throwback to the Egyptian Spotted Fishing cat, 2000
years extinct, but now believed to be a "ticked tabby." It is
a dotted tabby with chestnut color. It has the sleek grace
of a Siamese and has short hair with a smooth shiny coat.
It is a well-knit, large cat. The coloring is rich cream covered with chocolate or "chestnut" spots or dots, with bands
of chestnut on the throat, legs and tail. The eyes are golden,
the nose leather and pads are pink. They are sweet and
friendly.

THE PERSIAN

One of the best known and best established of the breeds,
the Persian is believed to have originated in Asia Minor.
This docile and ornamental breed was first recognized in
France and England in the 16th century.

A fine Persian should above all be boxy or what is known
as "cobby" in appearance, well proportioned and softly
rounded. The head should be square and must be in proper
proportion. The distance from the forehead to the nose
should be the same as from the nose to the chin. The cat
should also have a sweet, upcurling mouth. The jawbone
should be as wide as the top of the head. This all leads to
the square look. The cheeks should be full. The chin and
nose should line up perpendicularly. The nose should be flat
and as broad at the tip as at the base. There should be a
definite stop where the nose meets the forehead, known
as the break. The ears are small, round tipped, set slightly
forward, wide apart, not too large at the base and set even
with the corners of the eyes. They should also be covered
with a plush fur. The eyes are large, round, expressive,
and a brilliant color. The distance between the eyes should
be the same as the distance across each eye. The body
should be level with short legs, which are thick and strong.
The cat is muscular with a broad chest. The neck is short

Copper eyed white male Persian
Gr. Ch. Simbelair Fantastic
Sire: Ch. Skyways Rajah of Simbelair
Dam: Simbelair Pale Doll
Breeder/Owner: Mrs. S. Weston

and curved and broad. The tail is short and bushy in proportion in length to the body. It should be the same width from tip to base. The cat is large boned and heavily furred; the fur is flowing and silky. The frill around the

Chinchilla silver female Persian
Dbl. Gr. and Tr. Ch. Mer-C's Little Bit of Silver
Sire: Db. Gr. Bonavia Jester (Imp.)
Dam: Ch. Mer-C's Celeste
Photo: Nancy Meersman
Breeder/Owner: Dr. and Mrs. Eugene Couture

Odd eyed white Persian male
Gr. Ch. Simbelair Aristocrat
Sire: Ch. Skyways Rajah of Simbelair
Dam: Gr. Ch. Skyways Doll of Simbelair
Breeder: Mrs. S. Weston
Owner: Mrs. M. Myers

head and the ruff down the front of the cat and the tail should be full.

Standard Colors

BLUE EYED WHITE: The white is pure white and the eyes are a brilliant blue. No colored hairs should appear in the coat.

COPPER EYED WHITE: Brilliant copper eyes and a pure white coat.

ODD EYED WHITE: One blue eye and one copper eye. The fur is pure white.

Shaded silver Persian male
Gr. Ch. Walnut Hill Kaper of Sequoia
Sire: Gr. Ch. Walnut Hill Rondo
Dam: Walnut Hill Tiffany
Breeder: Mrs. Robert Weston
Photo: Elsa Lightner
Owner: Mrs. Albert Baccelli

BLACK: Jet black with color from roots to the tip of the fur. The eyes are orange or copper.

BLUE: Evenly colored with one level of tone color, without shading or markings from root to tip of hair. Eyes are copper or orange.

CREAM: One level shade of cream, sound to the roots. Cream is of an orangy hue. Eyes are copper or deep orange.

CHINCHILLA SILVER: Undercoat is pale silver or silvery white. Back, flanks, head and tail are tipped with jet black giving a sparkling silver appearance. Legs and face are

slightly shaded, but chin, ear tufts, stomach, and chest is
silvery white without tipping. Rims of the eyes and nose
is to be outlined in black and center of nose is brick red. It
has black footpads and its eyes are blue-green.

SHADED SILVER: Pure, unmarked silver shading gradually
down the sides, face and tail from dark on the ridge to
silvery white on the chin, chest, belly, and under the tail.
Legs are same tone as the face. The general effect should
be much darker than a Chinchilla silver. Eyes are blue-

Shell Cameo Persian male
Quad. Ch. Fergus's Shelley Boy of Theta
Sire: Gr. Ch. and Ch. Fergus's Honey Bear II
Dam: Fergus's Tonala
Breeder: Mrs. A. D. Fergus
Owner: Mr. and Mrs. Robert Wilson

green. Rims of eyes, lips and nose are outlined with black and center of nose is brick red. Foot-pads are black.

BLACK SMOKE: Jet black with a silvery white undercoat. Except for the silvery white frill and eartufts, the undercoat of the head, face, legs, back, sides, and tail do not show until the coat is parted. Belly and underside may appear grey, shading down to a silvery white. Eyes are deep orange or copper.

BLUE SMOKE: Appears blue (grey) with white or blue-white undercoat, dark blue points and mask, and a white or blue-white frill and ear tufts. Eyes are copper.

SHELL CAMEO: Ivory white ground color, frill, eartufts, shaded with red tipping on head, body, legs, back, and tail

Red tabby female Persian Spay
Premier Little Buttercup
Sire: Leigh's Rejie of Coppurry
Dam: Glen Moor's Dreamy
Breeder: Mrs. Roger A. Seebee
Owner: Mrs. Marian L. Newton

Brown tabby Persian female
Gr. Ch. Wynden's Holiday
Sire: Gr. Ch. Co-Mc's Lil Chess of Wynden
Dam: Gr. Ch. Bloenhill Fancy Free of Wynden
Breeder/Owner: Mrs. Ann Pevy

so as to give a sparkling peach glow to the cat. The eyes are copper.

SHADED CAMEO: Ivory white ground color, frill and ear-tufts, shaded more heavily on head, face, legs, body and tail, shading from dark on ridge to blend with pale ground color of undersides. Eyes should be copper or deep orange.

SMOKE CAMEO: So heavily tipped with red that it appears as a solid color. Lighter undersides and creamy white frill and eartufts. Ground color is pure white. This won't show until the coat is parted. The eyes are copper.

CLASSIC TABBY: Shows good contrast between pale

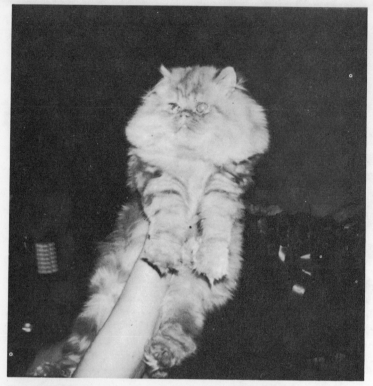

Red tabby Persian
Gr. Ch. Stonybrook Dristis
Owner: Mrs. Margaret English

ground color and deep heavy markings. Head is barred, with frown marks extending between the ears and down the shoulders, which divides the head lines from the spine. There is a butterfly on the shoulders. The back markings are distinctively wide: There is a dark center stripe with stripes of ground color on either side and these in turn are bordered by a darker secondary stripe. The dark swirls on cheeks and sides of the body should make a complete un-

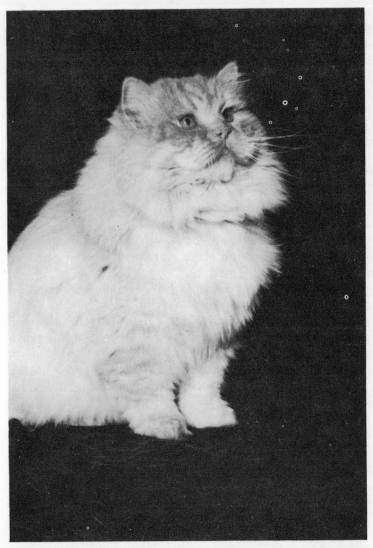

RM Gr. Ch. Fergus's Ginger Bear. Shaded Cameo Male
Breeder/Owner: Mrs. A. D. Fergus

broken color. Legs are evenly barred with bracelets coming to meet the body markings. The tail is evenly barred, with dark fluff.

MACKEREL TABBY: The marking is dense, clearly defined, and with narrow pencillings. Legs are evenly barred with narrows bracelets coming to meet the body markings. Head is barred with an M on the forehead. There are unbroken lines running back from the eyes, and lines running down the head to meet the shoulders. Spine lines run together to form a narrow saddle. Narrow pencilling runs around the body. The lip and chin are the same shade as the rings. Kittens have lighter chins.

BLUE TABBY: Ground color is icy blue white, with dense darker blue markings. Eyes are deep orange.

BROWN TABBY: Ground color, including lips and chin, a tawny brown with dense black markings. Eyes are a deep orange or copper.

BROWN MC TABBY: Same as brown tabby but mackerel markings.

CAMEO TABBY: Ground color of pale ivory broken with well-defined cameo (red or beige) markings in classic tabby pattern. Cameo markings are to be deeply tipped, but diminishing in intensity of color approaching roots of the hairs. Nose leather and pads are pink to beige. Eyes are gold to copper.

RED: Deep, rich clear red, free from shadings, markings or tickings and sound to the roots. Eyes are copper.

RED TABBY: Ground color is red with dense, darker red markings. Eyes are copper.

RED MC TABBY: Same color as red tabby but with mackerel markings.

SILVER TABBY: Ground color pure pale silver, decided jet black markings. Eyes are green.

SILVER MC TABBY: Same as silver tabby, but with mackerel markings.

CREAM TABBY: Ground color is pale cream with dense,

*RM Gr. Ch. Fergus's Prince Juba. Black Smoke Male
Breeder/Owner: Mrs. A. D. Fergus*

dark cream markings. Eye color is dark orange.

BLUE CREAM: Clear blue and cream should be well divided and broken into patches that are bright and well defined. Eyes are copper.

CALICO: White with unbrindled patches of black and red. White predominant on underparts. Eyes are copper.

TORTOISESHELL: Black with unbrindled patches of red and cream. Patches well defined and unbroken on both body and extremities. A blaze of red or cream on the face is desirable. Ears are copper.

PARTI-COLOR: White with unbrindled patches of black and white with unbrindled patches of blue or white with unbrindled patches of red or white with unbrindled patches of cream. Eyes are copper.

CAMEO TORTOISESHELL: White undercoat is silvery. Black or blue tipping and red or cream tipping are arranged in well-defined patches. Both silver and cameo markings are present on face, flanks, toes, and tail as well as back. A blaze on the face is desirable. Eye color to be orange or copper. Footpads either black or rose pink or combination of both.

PEKE FACE RED: Conforms in color and markings and general type to solid red or red tabby, but the head should resemble the Pekingese from which it gets its name. The nose is short and depressed or indented between the eyes. A wrinkled muzzle is prominent. Eyes are round, large, full, set wide apart and brilliant.

FAULTS: a long, narrow head; roman nose, thin muzzle, large, pointed ears; ears set together or off side; narrow chest, long back, long, thin neck; kinked tail, light boned, long legs, bowed legs, oval feet, extra toes, small eyes, green eyes on white cat, pale eye color.

THE REX

The Rex gets its name from the rex rabbit or *Castrorex,* as it was called in 1925. However, there the similarity ends. It is a selectively bred cat, but originally was a mutation in a domestic litter, first appearing in Cornwall, England, in 1950 (a cat called Kalli Bunker and owned by Mrs. Nina Ennismore). It came to be known as the Cornish Rex. It then appeared in Germany in 1951 (a cat named Lamm-chen and owned by Dr. R. Scheur-Karpin in East Berlin). In America two mutations occurred. The first was in 1953, Toni, owned by Mary Hedderman. The second was in 1959 when two rex were owned by Bob and Dell Smith of Roddell's cattery (Mystery Lady and Terry). This latter strain was continued under Mildred Stringham, with a cat named Kinky Marcella. In 1960 another mutation appeared in England (a cat named Kirlee, in Devon, owned by Mrs. Beryl Cox). This came to be known as the Devon Rex. Then Mrs. Frances Blancheri imported two Cornish rex, La-

Copper eyed white female rex
Gr. Ch. KatzenReich's Bianka
Sire: Hi-Fi's Forst
Dam: Gr. Ch. Katzenreich's Misha
Breeder/Owner: Bill and Madeline Beck
Photographer: Albert E. Allen

Mar Slos Dark Reflection
Owner: Margaret Slocum

Composite: Ch. d'Este Tedipus Rex II, Ch. d'Este Opus Rachel,
Gr. Ch. d'Este Quintessence of Rachel, d'Este Orator, Daz-zling
Galaxy of d'Este and d'Este Odyssey

morna Cove and Pendennis Castle. Since then breeding has
been carried on by Mabel and Charles Tracy of Paw Prints
Cattery, Mrs. Una Bailey of New Moon Cattery, and
Mrs. Helen Weiss of Daz-zling Cattery.

The Rex is characterized by its curly coat, which gives
the Rex cat the nickname of "poodle" cat. For this type
of cat to appear both parents must carry the Rex gene. It
is in this way that Rex cats are continually bred and have
become a natural breed. In the English Rex the down hairs
are half the normal length and thickness. In the German
Rex the awn and awn-down hairs exist, but the down hairs
are less numerous than in the English. Guard hairs are always absent. In general, the cat is rare and beautiful; it is
known to be affectionate, intelligent, brave, bold, with a

Blue female Rex
Gr. Ch. Rodell's Romona of Ristra
Sire: Ch. Rodell's Aristo
Dam: Som-Chai's Chloe
Breeder: Bob and Dell Smith
Owner: Richard Strain

Odd eyed white rex male
Gr. Ch. Rindy's Haven Nipper of Van Dol
Sire: Int. Ch. Daz-zling Icelus
Dam: Ch. Daz-zling Joyeus Noel of Rindy's Haven
Breeder: Mr. and Mrs. Ed. Rindfleisch
Owner: Mr. and Mrs. Virgil Nitz

sense of fun and easy to train. Though it appears delicate, it is of sturdy stock. While its body fur is dense and short, the middle coat is dense, fine, silky and has deep even waves. It has no guard hairs, but is all undercoat. The fur on the head and legs has a velvet feeling. The foreign Rex cats seem to be thinner and curlier. Even the whiskers on this cat are curly. The face is longer than it is broad, small and narrow. There is a break at the whiskers or muzzle, called a whisker break. The cheeks are lean. If the cat is well proportioned there is a straight line from the nose to the chin, the latter which appears firm and strong. The muzzle narrows to a rounded end and the neck is medium in length and slender. The ears are large, set high on the head, wide at the base, taller than wide and with a modified point at the tip. The ears are usually without fur. The eyes are medium in size, with at least one eye's width between them, oval in shape and slanted upward slightly. The body itself is small to medium, agile, long in proportion to the legs and slender. The tail is long and slender, tapering from body to the tip. The cat has heavy hips, a hard muscular body, and an arched back. It is, however, fine boned. The legs are muscular, particularly the hind ones, and long. The feet are dainty. Rexes come in many colors, much as the Persian.

FAULTS: wedge-shaped head, coarse hair, guard hairs, an abnormal tail (kinked or broken), and an open coat or bareness of coat.

THE RUSSIAN BLUE

The Russian Blue was believed to be similar to the ancient Egyptian cats. It comes from Northern Russia. It arrived in England in the late 19th century, brought there by Russian sailors. It first appeared in America in 1907.

This cat is long and graceful. It is also fine boned and of a light build. Its nose is medium long and upturned. The skull is flat, narrow with the forehead receding and curving into the back of the neck. The face is broad with a short wedge, not furred heavily and with an alert appearance. The eyes are oriental or almond shaped. They are set apart about one and one-half the eye's width. A vivid green is the eye color in a mature cat, although it may be green in kittens, then change to yellow, and then back to a green ring around the pupils. The legs are long and slender. The hind legs are slightly longer. The feet are small, neat and oval. The cat looks as if it is walking on tiptoe. The tail is straight

Russian Blue female Spay
Gr. Ch. Hengist Cassia of Rindy's Haven
Sire: Hengist Stroganoff
Dam: Hengist Saskia
Breeder: Mrs. Matasha Fiske, of England
Owner: Mr. and Mrs. Ed Rindfleisch

and tapering, long and thick at the base. The coat is fine, short, thick, dense, silken; and though it is close lying it stands up softly. This cat is silvery, particularly on the face. It is shy, gentle, friendly, alert, placid and likes humans. It is medium to dark blue. Its voice is sweet and soft. Guard hairs are silver tipped.

FAULTS: a kinked tail, the wrong number of toes and tabby markings.

THE SIAMESE

The Siamese, otherwise known as the Royal Cat of Siam, first showed up in Siam in the 19th century in a poem about cats with particular colors in the points and mask. They were sold to tourists by people who had stolen them from the Royal palace, where the cats resided. They made an appearance in England and France in the late 19th century. As a breed they are intelligent, childlike, alert, affectionate, sociable, and noted for their loud cry that can be mistaken for that of a baby. It is as insistent as it is loud.

They are a delicate-looking breed with elegant lines and delicate colors. Under the delicate look is a muscular body, firm and strong, giving an overall impression of a finely bred animal. They have slender, muscular, long and well-proportioned bodies, with delicate structure and dainty, oval-shaped feet. Its legs should be thin and of a medium length. The hind legs should be slightly longer, causing the body to slope to the neck. The tail is long and tapering, but proportionately thin all the way down in an even manner. The tail should also have a fine tip. Originally the Siamese had a kinked tail and was admired for this characteristic; but now a tail of that sort is not thought well of, and if a kink should appear at all it should appear only at the very end of the tail. A good type should have a triangular head: long, narrow, and wedge-shaped. The neck should be lean and strong looking. The cat has large ears, which should

Sealpoint male
Gr.+Tr. Ch. RM Quad. Ch. Sia Mews Tomoka of Kit Katz
Owner: Mrs. Hazel Cook

be long and wide at the base while pointed at the tip. The eyes should be almond-shaped and a brilliant, deep, vivid blue, almost the color of a sapphire. The distance between the eyes should be no less than the width of an eye. The nose should be long and straight with no break (the point where on some breeds the nose stops short at the forehead). The chin should be in line vertically with the tip of the nose. Siamese kittens are born white or pale, greyish

Male Lilac Point Siamese
Gr. Ch. Jo-San's Theseus
Sire: Quint. Ch. Sky Hill Tiger Cee of Finale
Dam: Tri. Ch. Jo-San's Persephone
Breeder/Owner: Mr. John Turner

cream and gradually the points appear. A dark mask (around the cheeks, eyes and mouth and up to the base of the ears) should develop. It should be a contrast to the paler main coat color. The cat should have a lighter coat on its underside than on the back. Points on the feet should be less dark than on the mask, tail, and legs. A second, less common type of Siamese—with a thicker coat, rounder head, larger type, and pale blue eyes—was once bred. These are not considered good for breeding in the cat world today.

A Siamese's coat is characteristically a short, glossy, fine-textured one that lies close to the body.

FAULTS: dark spots on the body, stripes anywhere on the cat, round eyes, white between the toes, a round head, a broad muzzle, a bulging forehead, pale eye color, a pinched look, a wide mouth, short, small ears; ears that are round tipped or set too close together, a cobby body, a short neck, short legs, a short, thick tail; light hairs in the points and a coarse, lusterless, shaggy, open coat. The Siamese comes in many different color points:

Color Points

LILAC POINT: The body has a pure white coat with no shading. The points are a frosty grey with a pinkish tone, a clear distinction from the blue point, which is much darker. The foot pads are lavender-pink, as is the nose leather.

CHOCOLATE POINT: The body is ivory white, with shadings (if any) the same color as the points. The points are a warm cinnamon or milk chocolate color. The mask in the kitten may be incomplete. The nose leather and foot pads should be pink.

SEAL POINT: The body is a cream or fawn, shading gradually into a lighter shade on the stomach and chest. The points are a deep seal brown. The nose leather and foot pads are the same color as the points. All points should be approximately the same color.

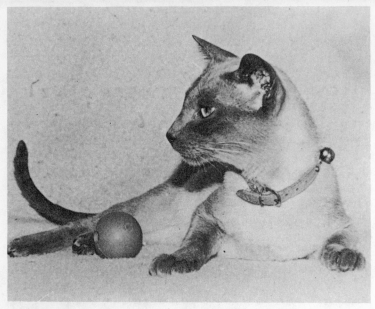

Blue Point Siamese
Gr. Ch. and RM Ch. Veja Sakda of Sand N' Sea
Breeder: S. J. McKendry
Owner: Mr. and Mrs. Charles L. Schmidt

BLUE POINT: The body is a platinum grey, which appears bluish and which shades into a lighter color on the belly and chest. The points are a deeper, greyish-blue color. All points should be as nearly the same as possible.

RED OR FLAME POINT: The body color is a cream white, shading to light orange, the same tone as the points. The points are a deep orange. This color point usually takes two years to develop. Foot pads and nose leather should be pink in this color point.

ALBINO POINT: The body is solid white. The eyes are clear pink with blue showing through. The foot leather and nose leather are both pink.

Other points that are possible are the Lynxpoint, the Torti Point and the Blue Cream Point. The first two are described under the Shorthair Colorpoint, the Blue Cream color is described in the section on Persians.

SHORTHAIR COLORPOINT

The type for this cat is the same as the Siamese. It is dainty, with tapering lines, sleek, muscular. The head has a long tapering wedge of medium size. The wedge starts at the nose and flares out in straight lines to the tips of the ears forming a triangle. There is no break at the whiskers. There should be no less than the width of an eye between the eyes. Bone structure of face is apparent. The neck is long and slender. The skull is flat, no bulge over the eyes, no dip in the nose, a straight line from the top of the head to the tip of the nose. The muzzle is fine and wedge-shaped. The chin is medium and the tip of the chin lines up with the tip of the nose in a vertical line. The jaw is receding and not massive. The ears are large, pointed, wide at the base, continuing the line of the wedge. The eyes are almond shaped or oriental and medium in size. They slant toward the nose, emphasizing the wedge. The eyes are never at the side of the head and are uncrossed. The body is medium, dainty, fine boned and with firm muscles. Shoulders and hips are in sleek lines. Hips are never wider than the shoulders. There is no flaring of lower ribs. The abdomen is tight. The legs are long and slim. The hind legs are higher than the front. The paws are small, oval, and dainty. The tail is long, thin, tapering to a fine point. The coat is short, fine, glossy and lies close to the body.

Colors

RED: Body is white with any shading the same tone as the points. The points are deep red on the mask, ears, legs, feet, tail. All should be dense and the same shade. The mask covers the face, including the whiskers connected to the ears by tracings. The leather and pads are the same color as the points. The eyes are blue.

TORTIE POINT (applies also to Himalayans), four varieties:

Standard Tortie: body even white or pale cream, shading gradually into a lighter color on the belly and shoulders and backs in older cats. Red or cream patches are a fault. The mask, ears, legs, feet and tail should be clearly defined in three colors. Cream and/or red preferred on all four feet, but two is acceptable. A blaze is desirable in the mask, preferably lower left and upper right jaw to have the same coloring. Absence of red patching in young adults. White toes or feet will disqualify, but cream or red patching is desirable. Nose leather is the same color as the cat. The paw pads, from pink to brown and patching of red or cream on feet, may extend into pad.

Lilac Point Tortie: Points frost grey or pinkish tone, with clear bright patches of cream. Lilac color predominates in all points, which are evenly matched. Color patching is restricted to the points. Shading is the same color as the points. Nose leather is lilac or clear pink; footpads are coral pink or clear pink or combination of both.

Blue Tortie Point: Known also as the blue cream point. Points in platinum grey or bluish tone. Patching is restricted to the points; clear patches of cream in coat; both colors in all points and blaze is desirable; no patches of color on body. Footpads and nose leather are dark blue-grey or clear pink or a combination of both. Ideally, they should be patched like the points.

Chocolate Tortie Point: The points are clearly warm milk chocolate with clear bright patches of cream. The chocolate is evenly matched in all points. Both colors should appear in all points. The nose is cinnamon or clear pink; foot pads are pink or a combination of both.

Seal Tortie Point: Points are deep seal brown with clear

*Quad. Ch. Keko's Flaming Arrow. Red Colorpoint
Breeder/Owner: Mr. and Mrs. Darrell W. Lewis*

bright patches of red and/or cream. Seal color should match in all points. Footpads and nose leather are deep brown or red-pink or a combination of both.

LYNXPOINT: (four varieties):

Lilac Point: Body has no stripes, mask has dark stripes vertically on the forehead, horizontally on the cheeks. There are dark spots on the whisker pad at base of whiskers. Ears are frosty grey with a thumb mark in a paler color at the back of the ears. The outer edges are lined in lighter color to a glacial white. Tufts on the ears are desirable. Nose leather is delicate lavender pink-rose, outlined in dark frost grey. There is a light brick to yellow colored area just above the nose leather. Paw pads correspond to the point colors. The legs are evenly barred with frosty grey bracelets. Paws resemble the mask in color. Webbing is lavender pink; there is a greyish pink matching the underside of the pads. The tail is glacial white with definite frosty grey bars. Tail must have solid frosty grey tip. Eyes are blue.

BLUE POINT: Body without markings, dark stripes vertical on forehead same as lilac point in description. Ears bluish grey with thumb mark in pale color. Outer edge is lined in bluish white. The leather is brick pink-red outlined in slate, with light brick to yellow above the nose leather. There are blue grey bracelets on the legs. The paws resemble the mask. Tail is bluish white with definite dark blue-grey bars. Tail must have a solid blue-grey tip.

CHOCOLATE POINT: Warm chocolate thumb mark. Outer edge lined in lighter chocolate to rich ivory. Warm in tone. Nose leather is cinnamon pink-rose outlined in dark chocolate. There is light brick to yellow above nose leather and there are chocolate bracelets. The webbing is warm chocolate. The tail is rich ivory with chocolate bars, and must have a solid chocolate tip.

Seal Point: Solid seal coloring masks the outer edge, lined with lighter greyish-fawn to cream. The leather is brick red outlined in black, and the webbing is warm seal. The tail is fawn with seal and with definite black or seal bars. The tail has a solid black tip.

2

Tender Loving Care

THE CAT'S HOME

Though the cat's home is also yours, you will find that your new addition will make it his castle; you may find yourself moving around him. There are a few things that you can do to make your cat feel at home when he arrives. If he is a show cat, you will, or should, decide at once not to let him run loose. This would be a danger to his health, as he may be more susceptible to disease if he is highly bred and any disease he contracts can then be brought back to other cats in the household. If your cat is a female, her roaming may result in her being bred by the local tomcat stud.

Your first step in making your cat feel at home is to establish a place for his toilet. This will consist of a box and absorbent litter. This is a special pebble-like substance derived from clay that is meant to be absorbent and cut down on odor. Kitty Litter is the best known brand. The box may be a fold out type purchased at any super market that you will fill with litter, purchased separately by the bag. One company sells its product in one complete package. As your cat gets bigger you will want to invest in a large, plastic-type box and buy your litter in the large, economy size bags. Some people use large dishpans; others treat their cats to a complete unit that consists of a large pan, an underplate to catch the litter dust, a large sifter for the removal of solids, and kitty deodorant. This type is an expense initially, but is supposed to be odorless and will last longer. It can be purchased from any company that specializes in cat products or from your local pet store. Without a doubt, this purchase is worthwhile, for as your kitten grows the smaller boxes of litter will be too small and more litter will be necessary as your cat will tend to become more odorous. Whatever your decision, you will need kitty deodorant and a scoop for solids. Do not, for your cat's sake, use Lysol or any other disinfectant or room deodorizer. They can be poisonous to the cat or at the least cause irritation to his eyes and nasal passages, particularly if they contain phenol. Use a kitty disinfectant and a kitty deodorant. There are many on the market, sold in pet stores or by specialty companies.

In addition, you will want your cat to have a special place of his own (if he is not caged). It is in this place that his box will be kept. This will usually be somewhere out of your way yet convenient for you to keep clean such as in the kitchen or bathroom (preferably the former). If you keep the box in the kitchen it will be handy for cleaning, and feeding your cat as well.

In addition to his box, he should always be able to find a dish of water and/or milk (the latter is not agreeable to the systems of some cats). At feeding time (whenever you decide this will be) the food dish will also be placed there. This is his spot. Keep it clean for him and do not change the location, as this will confuse him and may cause him to have accidents if he cannot find his box. You may find that no matter how hard you try, using newspapers to catch the flying litter and food dropped onto the floor, that he will continue to mess up the area in the same manner. For your home's sake and your cat's (they are basically clean animals and do not like things dirty or messy) clean the area each day and always clean out the water and food dishes after they have been used at each meal. The litter box should be cleaned out once a day and the box should be changed and (if of a washable substance) washed out at least once a week when you put in fresh litter. You will have to judge and it depends greatly on how many cats you have and how fast they dirty the box beyond the point where removing solids is enough.

When you first bring your cat home, introduce him to his special place; and, to insure housebreaking, show him where his box is. This is especially important after meals or when you find him sniffing around, particularly in corners, or beginning to squat. Place him immediately in his pan. He will be fast to get the idea, as cats are by nature clean and always use their box unless sick or confused. They will fastidiously cover their movements as it is second nature to them.

You may come across bad habits with which you will need to cope. If your cat is an annoyance at the table, only persistence on your part in putting him down will discourage him. Sometimes a tap with a newspaper will get the point across. It is painless, but the sound does bother cats. If your cat is clawing at the furniture you can try a scratching post, either purchased commercially or made yourself. They are simple to make by using a wooden base, a wooden log and covering the log with a piece of carpeting. The cat may use it, it is definitely up to him. Some definitely will not give it any consideration at all. Sometimes a clothes basket, a wicker hamper, or even a cardboard box is more to their liking. If distraction does not work, make the word "no" understood to your cat. Don't let anyone tell you that cats can't be trained and that they don't understand. They understand what they wish to and you can make them see what causes your displeasure as you would with a child. They want to please, though they may tease you a bit. Be persistent and let them know you are the boss (even if you wonder yourself sometimes).

On your part, take care of your cat by being sure (as you

would with young children) that no poisons, medications, disinfectants and other cleaning articles that could be poisonous to your cat are left where they can get access to them. Remember, cats are clever at getting into places you might think safe, especially if they think they will find something there to eat. Household plants, too, can be deadly to your cats if the cat chews the leaves or stems (and they seem to enjoy munching on plants for some unknown reason). Keep your plants out of reach if you do not want to give them up. Put them on a high shelf out of sight of the cat; or, if he can see it, at least make certain he cannot reach it. Remember, your cat's health is at stake.

If you are running a cattery you will need to make your cat's home more elaborate, either in your house or in a separate building, depending on your facilities. It is suggested that large cages be purchased. These should be collapsible for easy moving, with a floor underneath that will catch food and litter dropping from the cage. For ease in cleaning line it with contact paper (on the bottom) so that you can easily sweep it out and clean any places that are dirtied. A good product for disinfecting can be found in speciality houses selling cat supplies. Use only cat disinfectants when you clean out the cages and, again, cat deodorants. It is well to buy cages that have enough room for a cat to live there for some time. This is necessary if you have many cats and do not want them all running free at once. It also is handy when a cat is sick and you want him isolated from other cats. In this way he is out of reach of the other animals and can be given medication in his food (some will only take it this way) or special foods for his particular condition. Even if a cat is suffering from a mild problem like the runs, a cage can keep him from running around (upsetting his system further) and he can be given foods that are bland only, while the rest of the brood eats its usual diet.

Cages are also invaluable for breeding purposes. Your

male, once accustomed to his cage, will consider it his territory. For breeding purposes the cages with swingaway partitions are good for dividing the cage in half when breeding a female from outside your house is your aim. When the female in heat (the queen) is brought to you, put her in one side of the cage (which should by then be partitioned off) and let your male remain on his side. You may find your litter pans will not allow enough room for them to move around freely, so for this short period of time use disposable small boxes, and when the cage is opened fully again replace the regular pan. With the queen on one side and the stud on the other they can get used to each other without contact. She may be upset (she is upset anyway just by being in heat) with her new surroundings. She may be testy, aggressive and he may want to breed her but at the same time resent her intrusion. In this way they can move, calm down and get used to each other. This takes a day or so. When they are ready you can either open the partition (if the male will tolerate a female in his domain) or let them both out to breed.

As you can see, a cage is a versatile and valuable purchase. A final use for a cage is to keep your recently delivered female there to protect her from being bred again too soon if you have a male that roams freely. Or you can cage the male, letting him have short periods to run while she is caged. For a house with cats of two sexes or more than one breed, cages can be handy. If you have a cat family any larger than this, cages are a must. When using a cage or cages, acquaint your cat with his cage at an early age; if you don't he will get used to being free and may object to caging later. Place him in it for short periods and let him know it is his home. Place his pan, water, and food dish there and leave the door open for him to return at will or leave at will. You will find that as he gets used to it and grows up he will consider it his home—his territory.

You may want to train your cat to a harness and leash.

A standard collar is a poor idea, especially for a show cat. It mats the hair around the neck and may cause bare spots. There is, however, a good harness called the figure eight which has two loops. One goes around the neck; the other goes under the chest and front legs and across the shoulders. It is lightweight, does not cling to the fur, does not mat the hair, is comfortable; but your cat cannot escape from it.

CARE OF YOUR CAT

Clipping the Claws

It is well to keep your cat's claws clipped. It is not wise to have them removed or "declawed" (the correct expression). The declawing method is difficult on the cat and is unnecessary. The cat will never be showable in championship classes if he is declawed. In addition, the claws may grow back unnaturally, through the top of the paw, obviously a terrible ordeal for the animal. Even while the declawed paw is healing the cat must walk on the second digit, which is tender, as many nerves, tendons, and muscles have been disturbed by the operation. As you can see, it is risky, uncomfortable, and really quite unnecessary in comparison to the discomfort it causes the cat. The alternative is to learn how to clip your cat's nails correctly and keep them clipped as a natural and integral part of grooming. You should be careful in doing the job correctly. For this purpose you can buy a special pair of clippers which are meant to hold the nail and clip off just the right amount of nail cleanly without splintering or tearing. First in the procedure, take your cat's paw and hold it firmly with your fingers under the paw and your thumb on the top of the paw. With your fingers, push the foot pads firmly until the nails come out of their sheaths. Then with your thumb on top of the paw put pressure down on the paw to hold the nails out. Now, notice where the white of the claw ends and the pink begins. You do not want to cut near the pink. It is here that the blood flows in the claw. Always cut below the pink; if you cut above it (and into it) the nail will bleed and the cat will be subjected to discomfort. Begin doing this procedure when the cat is first a kitten to accustom him to the procedure and to keep his nails dull, thus forcing him to jump rather than claw his way up the furniture. This develops his jumping and saves your furniture. In addition, if the claws are dull then fighting between two cats (or even rough playing) should not cause as much damage, particularly in the sensitive and crucial eye area.

Handling Your Cat

Take care when you handle your cat. Begin when he is a kitten. A cat should never be lifted by the scruff of the neck (despite what the mother cat does). Always lift using both hands. There are two ways to lift. The most common is to place your right hand (reverse if you are left handed) under, and in front of, the cat's front paws and legs. With your left hand support the cat's hind end. In this way the cat is well supported. If you are uncertain of the cat's disposition, it is best to keep your hands away from where the cat can get at them. Use your right hand and grasp the cat by the scruff of the neck and at the same time put your left hand under the cat's hind end. In this way, the cat is still supported; but he cannot get at your hand if he is feeling frisky.

Traveling with Your Cat

When your cat goes traveling he deserves special consideration. His need to travel will probably be limited to trips to the vet (some routine, some for sickness), trips with your family, and trips to shows. I imagine that you have seen cats riding on the back shelves of cars, or sitting on top of a car seat balancing expertly. Many cats love to travel and do so with real grace. However, even the best traveler and the most experienced balancer can be hurt if he loses his balance (as when the car stops short). This is a definite danger to the cat and can also upset the driver. There are other cats who are slightly afraid of traveling and, if allowed to roam the car freely, will hide under the seat, if you are lucky. Others prefer to find comfort and security at your feet and, if you happen to be the driver, this presents a very dangerous situation. Because of these factors, it is best to invest in a carrier for your cat. These can be purchased through mail order houses or at a local pet store. They come in handy for taking the cat to the vet's, on trips with you or to shows. I recommend a carrier with small air holes that allow adequate ventilation. You can choose from many varieties. Some allow you to place your cat in from the top (the suitcase variety) and some with a door on the side from which the cat makes his entrances and exits. Some carriers are wooden with open, wire-covered areas through which the cat can peer out and you can peer in to check on him. These are commonly used by the airlines in shipping animals. Others are made of a heavy material with a similar opening covered with wire. These tend to be less heavy because of the material used to build them. If you do choose a model with the wired-over opening, do get one that has a cloth flap that fits over the opening securely and is anchored firmly with snaps. This is handy for two reasons. It allows you to totally enclose the cat (except for the air holes in the side) in case he gets upset. Sometimes enclosing him gives him a sense of security. You can unsnap the flap at any time to check on him. Another good concept of this type of carrier is that the flap, when anchored over the wire opening, cuts out drafts that can give your cat a chill. There are other carriers with plastic windows through which the cat can peer and you can check on him. This type cuts down on any drafts completely. Whatever your choice, be sure the carrier affords enough room for the cat and perhaps even for his litter pan if the journey is to be a long one. These carriers also provide you with a comfortable handle for ease in carrying. It is not a good idea to put anything into the carrier that the cat can wet on, because spending time with the damp article can lead to a case of the sniffles.

Shipping a Cat

When shipping a cat, which will occur when you are selling to another party who is too far away to pick the cat up in person, be sure to check with the people who will ship the cat. There are several reasons for doing so: You will want to know the cat's departure time in order to let the party waiting to receive him know when he is leaving. Also check on the expected arrival time. Naturally, you should let the new owners know this, as they will of course want to be there on time to avoid letting the cat spend more time than necessary in his carrier, especially after a long, perhaps frightening, trip.

You may want to put some dry food that will not spoil into the carrier. You will also want to know the shipping charges. These can be paid to you by the new owners before the cat is shipped. Otherwise, you can send the cat C.O.D. and the new owner will pay when the cat arrives. If you find out the charges you can let the new owners know what to expect in the way of shipping costs.

You have a choice as to the type of carrier your cat will be shipped in. Sometimes the new buyer may prefer to ship you a carrier to use. Otherwise, you may buy one—at the new owner's expense—and ship in that. Another possibility is to buy ones provided by the shipper; this can be paid for along with the shipping charges at the point of arrival. To repeat, be sure you caution the new owners to pick the cat up immediately upon arrival. He will have had a long trip and he has a new home to adjust to. Do not let him wait needlessly for someone to come for him.

Grooming

This is essential to your cat's looks and well-being—especially essential if he is a show animal. Before you begin grooming you must decide two things. The first one is about your cat. Will he take to grooming easily? If the answer is "no," then plan to have someone on hand to help you. This is easy if your cat venture is a partnership or a husband-and-wife operation. The second thing you should do is set aside a definite time for grooming each day. As with routine tasks, they are easily forgotten or set aside for other things if not made part of your daily routine. If a cat is not groomed daily, he will not look or feel at his best. In addition, mats and tangles will accumulate, and when grooming does take place it is doubly hard on both you and the cat. He will be less happy about grooming if it is a difficult thing for him to go through.

You will probably groom your cat more often and more meticulously starting a week before a show. If you have a cat that is high strung another person can be helpful—in fact almost necessary—for holding the cat. The front paws and head can be controlled with one hand, while the other hand can hold the back paws. Sometimes, with an especially excited animal, gloves (such as those heavy padded ones used in gardening) can be useful. A last resort is to bundle a frisky cat in a blanket, leaving uncovered only the area being worked on at the time. Tranquilizers can be used, but consult your vet first. If all else fails the vet can do the grooming for you. This should not be necessary if the cat is done daily.

Grooming is not uncomfortable for the cat. A suggestion that breeders give to people buying their kittens (and, of course, follow themselves while the kittens are still in their charge) is to begin daily grooming in kittenhood so that when the cat becomes older he is used to (and even enjoys) his daily grooming. If started early, mats and tangles need not develop; and the cat will always enjoy grooming as much as he does being petted.

The first step in grooming is the ears. Using cotton balls

or Q-tips with baby oil, check for mites. Go gently and do not probe too deeply or be too rough. Avoid trouble spots, which are best left to heal by themselves. Next take a piece of cotton, and, with water or boric acid solution carefully clean the area under the cat's eyes where ooze may have left unsightly patches of crust. Now you are ready to begin on the body of the cat. Remember, you want to preserve your cat's fur and its luster. Your purpose is to stimulate the scalp and rid the cat of dead hair which is detracting from his looks and collecting dirt and oil. You do not want to remove good hair, nor do you want to mat or tangle the hair (particularly in the long haired cat). Your aim is to keep him clean so that actual baths will be kept to a minimum. Baths tend to make the fur less lustrous and dryer.

Your first step is to use a show coat cleaner or dry shampoo to demove deeply embedded dirt. Concentrate on the areas where oils accumulate and dirt along with it. Soak a cloth in the solution or dust on the dry shampoo; apply it against the lay of the hair to remove embedded dirt. With the show cleaner a spray may be used, but the noise sometimes frightens the cat. These pleasant smelling shampoos enhance the coat and keep it clean.

When the cat is fully wet or dusted, apply the cleaner with a brush. Then, lay the hair back in place again. Pay particular attention to the stomach hair (do that first), the area at the base of the tail (particularly in the male), behind and in front of the ears, on the inside of the legs, on the chest and chin, and the back of the hind legs (where cats sit on their haunches). Now look for matted areas. A rake tool will do well here on small tangles. It is wise not to resort to the scissors as this will give a chopped-away look and the fur may not grow back evenly. Comb through firmly with the rake and you will find that mostly deep, clumped hair will be removed. When hair dies it usually is no longer rooted well and should come out easily.

On longhairs concentrate on the insides of the back legs, the stomach, and the outer edge of the tail. In a longhair the tail should not be groomed daily, but only as needed so as to maintain its fullness. If mats and tangles are particularly thick you may find a splitter, consisting of a razor and guard, is safe for the cat and you. Hind areas tend to accumulate this type of matting because loose movements and litter stick to the fur and clumps. This tool will split the tangle just enough to make the rake useful. Once all the tangles and mats are removed you can comb through the fur using a comb with metal teeth that will catch small clumps of dead hair missed by the rake. There are numerous types of this comb available. They vary as to shape and type of handle. Those with the teeth fairly close together are the best.

On shorthairs, smooth out the coat with a clean cloth, rubbing down the hair firmly to produce a smooth, glossy coat. On the longhair, fluff up the coat with a pin or wire brush, concentrating on the tail, the ruff (the hair around the neck, which should be brushed up and out into a halo around the throat), on the stomach and around the backs of the ears to match the ruff. If you feel you cannot handle grooming by yourself ask your vet for help, particularly if your cat is badly tangled and matted. After grooming is finished, apply snow white show powder (particularly in preparation for a show) and each day brush out a little. This powder will keep down the oils and, in that way, the dirt accumulation that takes the luster out of the coat of the cat.

The Bath

When your cat has become so dirty that a bath is warranted you have two alternatives. You can take your cat to the vet or you can do it yourself. There is a problem in bathing too often and it should not be necessary unless your cat gets into something he shouldn't. Unfortunately, all shampoos, even those especially for cats, can't help but take some of the life and luster out of the cat's fur. If the bath is in preparation for the show, do it a week before to allow time for the coat to regain its full life. Your day to day grooming should make a bath unnecessary except in extreme cases. You will find that with the male, the tail presents a place where a shampooing must be resorted to. This problem is called "stud tail" and at the base of the tail an oil seems to accumulate that rapidly collects dirt and dust. The result is a greasy, dirty, and generally unsightly tail that you would never allow on a cat going into a show ring. This area calls for a cleaning agent that will break up the oil. Any shampoo will take out the dirt, but when you have dried the cat you may find the hairs still stand out and still look and feel greasy. For this problem some people use baby oil, rubbing it in and then shampooing it out. I have found that a mild detergent will also do the job. Pay particular attention to this spot in bathing your cat.

Have the items you will need handy before you begin to bathe the cat. The following will come in handy during the bath: at least three large towels, Q-tips or cotton balls, baby oil or a mild detergent, a washcloth, a cup, a large pitcher, mineral oil or boric-acid solution, and whatever shampoo (baby or cat shampoo) that you decide to use. In addition, enlist the services of someone to help you hold the cat while you do the bathing.

First, clip the cat's claws as already described. Then, using the cotton or Q-tips and mineral oil or plain water, be sure the ears are free of mites and dirt. Next, clean your cat's eyes with boric acid solution and put a drop of this solution or mineral oil in each eye in case soap should get in them. This will cut down on irritation. The area under the eyes should be cleaned using cotton balls and water to get off the crusty patches that accumulate there.

Then draw the bath, using lukewarm water. You could compare bathing a cat to bathing a baby. Much of the procedure is the same. Test the water with your wrist and

remember to only fill the sink or tub an inch or two. Put
the cat into the water and allow him to calm down. Work
from the head back, using the cup to wet the head. Tilt the
cat's head back, so water will not run into his eyes. Wash his
face with the washcloth. Then, using the pitcher, completely
soak down the cat's body. When you use the shampoo, use
it only where it is needed. This will probably be, if your day-
to-day care has been good, only the area behind and in front
of the ears (where oil accumulates), on the paws, and particularly on the hind legs where the cat sits, on the underside where longhairs especially brush their fur on dusty
floors or furniture, and finally on the tail where the largest
amount of oil accumulation occurs. When you have covered
all the areas you need to, use the cup to rinse away soap
from the head area. Again, be sure to tilt back the cat's
head to keep soap out of the eyes. Then use the pitcher and
fresh water to fully soak the cat with water, repeating until
you have all the soap out of the fur. If the soap is all out
the fur will not feel slippery at all, but will seem to squeak.
Be sure to check the areas where you concentrated the soap.
If any soap is left, dirt will accumulate there rapidly and
undo your job. Use the washcloth to get soap and water off
the cat's face. Hopefully you have only shampooed where
needed and not on the areas where oil and dirt are not evi-
dent. A spray may be used in this rinsing process, but the
sound and force may scare the cat.

When you are sure you have gotten all the soap out, place
a towel on a flat surface—a counter, the floor, or a vanity.
Rub the cat down firmly to squeeze out excess water and then
place the cat on the towel. Quickly place another towel
around him and rub firmly to get out more water. When
you think he is fairly free of water let him out of the now
damp towels and let him shake himself good. You'll have
to endure the spray; he's been through much more. Then
take the third towel and rub briskly until the cat is damp dry.
He will be ready now to run and hide, to lick himself dry

and just to get away from you who have subjected him to the ordeal. You may want to resort to more drying by using a hairdryer or a vacuum cleaner, but a draft is never advisable for a cat. It is best to turn the heat up in the house, keep him out of drafts and let him lick himself dry as he will usually instinctively do. In an hour or so he will be fluffy or sleek (depending on the length of his fur) and clean. A job well done.

When the bath is complete and the cat is thoroughly dried, powder the cat well. Daily brush out the powder, leaving a beautiful, clean and lustrous coat. This show powder is used to keep down oils and the dirt it attracts. It is also used to brighten white coats. It is not wise to take the powder to a show or use it there. It does little good at that late date and the judges (should you not get all the powder out) will frown greatly on a cat that has been powdered in an effort to give a false impression of whiteness.

You may find that the stud tail on your male is especially stubborn. Wait a day and then wash only that area again, using mild soap or the baby oil method. Again, rinse well and be sure there is no soap left in. With persistence the stud tail can be eliminated.

A word of advice: do not let the stud tail get out of hand in the first place. Wash this spot when trouble first appears—one washing should do the trick.

FEEDING YOUR CAT

There are certain general rules of feeding your cat or kitten that should be observed, for his sake. To prevent indigestion, all foods should be served at room temperature, not from the stove or from the refrigerator. A cat also prefers to eat in peace and quiet. If he is not in a cage when being fed, keep children away from him and don't let adults pet him at this time. Cats also prefer dishes that are shallow, making their food easy to get at. They will enjoy pieces of food that are small enough to chew easily, but large enough to get their teeth into. You should always serve each meal on a clean plate. Cats are fastidious and besides, you don't want food left out too long on a plate. Food that is left for a long period of time will tend to harden, making your job harder when it comes time to wash out the dish. If you must serve on a flat dish, put the food at the edge to allow the cat easy access.

If your cat is a new arrival, allow him to adjust to his environment by not expecting him to make too many changes at once. Find out what he has been eating and serve that until he is settled in. When he seems adjusted to his new environment, feed him what you usually feed your cats. Sometimes what you want your cat to eat and what he wants to eat are two different things. Compromise can be tried, or you can hold out until he is hungry enough to eat what you know is best for him. Some cats are just stubborn enough to outlast you; they are, indeed, individuals. For example, in our family (we consider our cats part of the family) we have one Persian who insists on drinking milk whenever she can (usually sneaking up on the table when my back is turned to sip out of the baby's cup). The problem is two-fold. The baby doesn't appreciate this (nor do I) and milk is completely unpalatable to this cat's system. She will immediately get the runs. We have learned that cottage cheese or egg yolks on occasion is a good compromise. Another cat wolfs down all the meat, without chewing, leaving little for the rest. Sometimes the result is a loss of the entire meal because she is such a glutton. Now she is fed in a cage where she gets only what she needs and she now has learned to eat more slowly and we have no more troubles with her losing her dinner. Our first cat still feels she should be our first and *only* and she plainly refuses to eat with the others at all, but waits until they are finished and humbly eats the remains. What a martyr! She is also one who prefers what we eat and is hard to persuade that chicken chow mein should not be part of her diet.

Because cats are individuals they will have their own likes and dislikes; we know both what is best for them and what they like. We try to give them a little of both without giving them anything that is bad for their digestion. Water should always be left down for your cat and should be kept fresh. It is well to remember that cats are sometimes slow eaters, so give them enough time to finish their meals. After you are sure they have finished, remove their food dishes. Dry food can be left out for them to nibble on, but I caution against too much of this diet as any dry food and even some canned cat and dog foods are high in ash and calcium. This can lead to the serious problems of stones in the urinary tract that will cause discomfort and can lead to worse problems which will be discussed later.

All cat food should be supplemented to some extent with vitamins, particularly if you are serving canned cat food. Do not serve your cat fancy or spicy foods. They hardly ever care for them and they are often bad for digestion. Avoid certain types of bones like fish, chicken and chop bones. These bones are easily splintered and have sharp edges which can cause internal damage.

Don't overfeed your cat; if you have a "fat cat" have him checked by a vet and given a good diet. Any vegetable that is starchy will be indigestible unless cooked and mashed. In addition, fish should be cooked. All other foods are served raw. Liver should be browned slightly, and it should not be given in large quantities as it has a laxative effect. Aside from what your cat likes and how he likes to eat it, notice the general peculiarities of the cat regarding food. Some of these idiosyncrasies can be allowed and are even good for them; others may be bad for them and still others are just nonessential. I have seen cats slurp tomato juice (good for them as it does contain vitamin C), eat olives (they prefer black ones), gulp donuts, cake, and generally anything sweet. Italian food is very popular with some cats, probably because of the tomato sauce. Potato chips are popular, though they are usually licked for the salt and seldom completely eaten. Mayonnaise is a real favorite, probably because of the egg content. All of these may be to your cat's liking and if your cat roams the house freely, they are sometimes accessible. However, a steady diet of table scraps and nibbles from your snacks will not help develop a well proportioned, healthy animal. Indulge him occasionally if you wish, but normally stick to the diet you have chosen.

Generally, cats should have a high-protein, high-fat diet with vitamins. The latter should include B-1, B-12 and B complex; also vitamins C, E, and D are essential. Of those above, B-12 is important to give more red blood cells and D is necessary to assimilate calcium, which can be another cause of stones in the urinary tract. In the meat or protein department, fresh meat is the best source of protein. Liver is popular because of its strong smell and taste. However, too much can cause a case of the runs. This will dehydrate the cat and leave him with little nutritional value in his system. Kidney of all kinds is good. Fish, tripe, and all muscle meat—whether it is chicken, beef or lamb—is good. Spicy meats, such as ham and sausage, are not recommended, because they are hard to digest.

For additional protein, milk is good, especially for kittens. However, in adult cats it can cause loose movements. A substitute can be cheese which is a cat favorite and seems to be more binding. Eggs are good, but give only the yolk. The white is hard to digest. If eggs are cooked, as they should be with kittens, the white becomes more digestible. Vegetables too can be given in the daily diet, but be sure and cook those that are starchy. Spinach, carrots, and string beans are recommended for their nutritional value.

The subject of canned cat foods is an important one. If you do decide to rely on them (and they are less expensive and easier to serve than a mixed diet of your own) please do not forget to supplement the food with vitamins. The way to choose the best canned cat food—and dog food is really a better choice as it is higher in food value—is to check for the one with the highest protein percentage and lowest calcium and ash content. The vitamins in these canned foods are minimal, so again use supplements. While we are on the subject of vitamin supplements, there are many on the market. You can buy separately, B-12, B-complex, prenatal supplements or you can buy products like Pervinal or Theralin which are both high potency vitamin mineral supplements. These will build up the cat physically and make him feel better. In addition, there are products like Linatone which are for the skin and coat of the cat, but which also contain some vitamins. This product prevents shedding, flaky skin, dull coats and scratching due to all these problems. You may decide to use common brewer's yeast (Vitamin B) and cod liver oil (Vitamins A and D). The latter does wonders for the condition of your pet's coat.

As your cat changes, so will his (or her) diet. A kitten eats differently from an adult cat, a mother cat has a different diet—or at least more abundant diet—and an old or fat cat must have a diet suited to his needs. Kittens, for example, should be fed four or five times a day. A morning meal should include cereal (baby cereal or Pablum) and some milk. Noon and evening meals contain chopped meat, milk, and vitamin supplements. Vegetables should be added to one of these meals. It is wise and easier for you to use baby strained meat with your kittens and even the strained vegetables. The food value is still there, but it is easy to serve, requires no preparation, and is easy for the cat to eat. A fourth meal may contain both meat and vegetables, plus vitamins and milk. Whether or not a fifth meal is given is up to you. You can tell how much your cats need and if a fifth meal is really needed. All meals should include milk. You may use evaporated milk diluted, half and half, with water. Remember to serve all food at room temperature. You wouldn't give a baby a cold bottle. Kittens are much like babies in many ways.

The above menu is meant for weaning. Before this time the mother will of course feed the kittens. All foods after milk should be introduced gradually and one at a time; first add cereal with milk, then strained vegetables, and finally strained meat. Finally, you will serve larger bits of vegetables and meats and graduate the kitten to a cat diet. The meals will get larger, but less frequent, until the kitten is a cat.

Cats differ in their needs and wants. Some like numerous small meals; others like few large meals. As a suggestion the following is the diet I have found my cats thrive on. High protein cereal is used as a base (this is baby cereal) and mixed with warm water. Cooked mixed vegetables are added. Vitamin supplements are added at one meal a day. Then, large chunks of meat are mixed in and the entire mixture is stirred together. The meat is sometimes kidney, sometimes stew meat, and sometimes chicken. Liver is a special treat, never a constant meat diet. A few times a week cottage cheese or egg yolk is added to the mixture. However, too much protein can be as bad as too little. If a cat gets the runs we isolate him and serve only cottage cheese. It is a favorite and seems to be bland enough to control digestive troubles. So far, it has worked very well. Between meals we leave out small quantities of dry cat vittles for them to chew on. It is served in safe quantities and is good for their teeth and gums.

In a pregnant cat dairy products should be increased and the cat's meals, in general, should be larger. She is eating for quite a few and her condition will deteriorate if she is not fed well during her pregnancy. Remember too to give the pregnant cat pre-natal supplement vitamins.

An altered cat is another story. Keep his food consumption down, as he will tend to get heavy faster than an unaltered cat. Speculation on why this occurs is heavy itself, but whether it is because of a change in body chemistry or just because the cat is not as likely to be active, they do tend to eat more and put on weight. Another problem in altered cats, males particularly, is urinary stones. Keep his diet low in ash and calcium to avoid the possibility of this condition.

Old cats are a particular problem in that they have almost reverted back to the needs of a kitten. They are plagued by sensitive nerves and ears (let them eat in peace), circulatory problems, chronic sinusitis which makes it hard for them to breathe, poor digestion, tartar on the teeth, and gingivitis (an inflammation of the gums) which results in bad breath and intestinal problems. Feed this older cat food that is easily digested and easily chewed. Fine, well-chopped food and strained vegetables, again in addition to cereal, aid in chewing and digesting. Vitamins are essential, for his body will need all the outside help it can get. Try to encourage him to chew some meat or some hard food in order to keep his teeth and gums active to some degree and to help the cat resist degeneration as long as possible. Finally, if your cat is getting fat, get him to a vet for a check-up and a good diet. Remember, a fat cat will not live so long as a well-proportioned one because the strain on the body is greater with every ounce of unnecessary fat.

LOVING CARE VERSUS CRUELTY TO CATS

It would be a mistake to close the chapter on care for your cat without discussing the sad conditions that do prevail where cats are not given tender loving care. The Pet Pride organization, whose aim is healthy and happy cats, establishes seven serious sins that are perpetrated against cats. Do not be guilty of any of these:

1. *Allowing cats to be used for laboratory experiments.* This can occur when a cat is considered unmanageable by his owner, no longer wanted in the home, unable to be sold, unbreedable, unshowable and when no good home can be found. The cat is then sent to the local pound, where the

owner tells himself the cat will receive a home or at worst be mercifully put to sleep. Indeed, this often happens. But sometimes these pounds will sell such cats to scientific laboratories, where they are used in experiments—a cruelty to the poor cat that is inexcusable. It is true that these experiments are done to help find cures for illnesses. The scientists' motives are pure, but cats are not the proper instrument for such experimentation.

2. *Over-population* has also struck the cat world in the form of males who roam the street breeding females and leaving behind kittens who in turn carry on this process. These are homeless animals and are basically not happy in their free roaming condition. They contribute to the public's general feeling that cats are a problem to be eliminated as quickly as possible. This is an unfortunate opinion as cats are intelligent, loving animals that should be bred with care and then passed on to a home where they will receive the love and attention they need and desire. Even some breeders can be guilty of this overpopulation. They are too anxious to sell kittens and thus breed too often, selling kittens too young, at too low a price, and sometimes without the necessary shots which could have cut down on unnecessary deaths of the feline community. Not only is this unfair to the kittens, who rarely fair well or receive the type homes they should, but these breeders are in fact downgrading their breed.

3. *Catteries that house their cats continuously in cages,* not allowing them their right to exercise periods and tender loving care, are perpetrating a crime against these cats. It is not enough for a cat to go to show, sire, be bred and then return to its cage without human kindness and a chance to run and play and live a full, happy life.

4. *Physical neglect* is another sin which often occurs through lack of proper information (one of the reasons for

books like this). Sometimes the sin is due to neglect or laziness. Some cats are not given their necessary shots, so that they die of such conditions as Feline Enteritis (distemper). This is a crime, as cures and preventions for these conditions are available. It is bad enough that some conditions cannot be avoided or cured and we owe much to the Morris Animal Foundation, which is dedicated to the cause of finding preventives and cures for feline diseases. There are cats which suffer with ear mites, fleas, worms, fungus, hairballs, and mats—which cause them discomfort and make them feel unattractive and unloved. A good cat owner will not allow these conditions to escape his eye, but will watch for them and rid the cat of them as soon as they are discovered.

5. *Leaving cats alone for long periods* of time to fend for themselves (whether inside or out) is unfair and cruel. Throwing a cat out to find his own way, especially after he has been accustomed to care, is inexcusable.

6. *Declawing a cat* is not only cruel, it is unnatural, painful, unnecessary, and a convenience for the owner at the expense of the cat.

7. *Breeding for money and forgetting the cat's welfare* is a final cruelty. Money should never be the driving force which directs people into the cat business. Cat owners and breeders should be willing to give love, attention, and freedom to roam. They may be caged, but they should always be allowed exercise periods and a time with their owners for the affection they need and deserve. Cats that are bred too often for financial gain are being exploited in the cheapest way. Give your mother cat a rest between litters for her health and well-being. A female should be bred a maximum of twice a year. If you are a true cat lover, money is your last concern when it comes to your cat's happiness, and his health is, or should be, your first.

SUPPLIES AND EQUIPMENT TO HAVE ON HAND

Nail Clippers
A Scratching Post
Shallow Cat Dishes
Litter Boxes or Pans
Kitty Litter
Kitty Toys
Kitty Deodorant
Water Dish
Cat Bed
Metal Comb
Wire Brush
Soft Brush
Q-Tips
Cotton Balls
Coat Conditioner—Linatone
Small Cup
Large Towels
Face Cloth

Dry Shampoo
Spray Bottle for Show Cleaner
Show Cleaner
Snow White Powder
Rake Comb
Carrier(s)
Harness Collar
Tangle Splitter
Cat/Baby Shampoo
Ivory Soap
Cage(s)
Kitty Litter Scoop
Tabby Deodorant
Boric Acid Ointment or Solution
Mineral Oil
Vitamin Supplements—Pervaline or Theraline

3

To Your Health

THE WELL CAT

A healthy cat has certain characteristics lacking in a sick cat. Your cat, when in good health, will want to play and will be alert to every movement. His appetite will be good and he will, as usual, remind you when it is dinnertime. Usually any indication on your part that food is being prepared will bring him running. His eyes will shine and will be clear, following any moving object with intense interest. His bowel movements will be well formed and he will eliminate at least once a day without any difficulty. The coat of a healthy cat is smooth and shiny, soft and unbroken. He will not only seek you out to play, but will also seek out and respond to your affection. He will purr when petted as if to thank you for your care and attention. His normal temperature will be 100-102.5 F. A healthy cat should have no odor to his breath, unless he has just eaten strong food. The cat's mouth should be clean and the gums pink and healthy.

THE SICK CAT

If you are aware of your cat at all, you will notice when it is sick. He may no longer wish to play or be fondled, but will lie around listlessly. Vomiting is a definite sign of sickness, particularly if it is yellow and occurs between meals.

This is very different from the immediate rejection of food that is too cold or too hot or eaten too fast that occurs immediately after eating. Hairballs can cause vomiting, but the hairball should be visible after the cat gags. Also, this type of vomiting is not persistent. A cat's appetite will reflect his bad health. A sick cat willl not wish to eat or may have difficulty in swallowing. Some sick cats may drink large quantities of water, while other sick cats attempt to drink but cannot. A cat's bowels should be neither too firm (from a strained movement) or too loose. His urine should not be dark or strong smelling; it should not show traces of blood. Any sign of difficulty in eliminating urine or feces points to trouble. Any temperature should be considered an indication of trouble. A sick cat will not look well. The coat may be broken, dry, coarse to the touch or too oily causing it to stand out in places as if the hair were stuck together.

Shedding is a sign that something is wrong. Often sickness will show up in persistent sneezing, red eyeballs, discharge from the eyes, a runny nose or eyes. The cause may be minor. An occasional sneeze may be an allergy, but if it persists or is constant it may be more serious. The mouth should not give off an offensive odor, nor should the gums be red, swollen or irritated or pale. Any scratching or pawing at an area may indicate irritation. Swellings and sores should always be investigated. The worst sign is a cat that only sits with his head over a dish of water, unable to drink. Get this cat to a vet!

HOW TO TAKE THE TEMPERATURE

Again, the procedure is similar to that used when taking a baby's temperature. A normal, rectal thermometer will do the job. Another person is necessary to hold the cat while you do the actual job. Grease the thermometer with baby oil or vaseline and gently insert it into the rectum about an inch and a half. Hold it there for three minutes.

MINOR ILLNESSES

Parasites

The first type of minor ills takes into account all forms of outside organisms which can cause trouble for your cat. The first type of parasite is the common FLEA. Fleas will, of course, prefer cats or dogs to people and will come into the house on the animals. They can, however, come in on the clothing of people and will attack them if an animal is not available. Their presence is usually signalled by scratching and pawing on the part of the cat. You can see their presence either by the small, tiny black fleas themselves or their black, gritty substance called flea dirt. These are blood-sucking creatures and can cause your cat discomfort and drain his energy. There are numerous ways to get rid of them, but they can be persistent. You can wash what is washable, including your cat. Vacuum what isn't washable. One trick to be sure and kill them is to put flea powder in the vacuum bag first. There are powders that can be used on the cat by sprinkling it on and rubbing it into the coat. You should concentrate on the head, neck, and tail particularly. In addition, there are soaps to wash the cat with, sprays and solutions which are all safe for the cat and, hopefully, deadly for the flea. Fleas will breed if not stopped. The eggs drop off the cat and their larvae hatch in and around the home. When they mature, they rejoin the poor cat. If all else fails, put the cat out of harm's reach and get professional help to exterminate them.

TICKS are another type of parasite that will enjoy living on your cat. They are usually picked up in bushes and carried into the house on the cat or on the clothing of a human. They attack the ears of the cat and can cause infection and abscesses. They also attack the skin and are usually found on the head and neck. They will bury their heads under the cat's skin, leaving their tail sticking out. Like fleas, they are blood sucking parasites. You can get them out by pulling them out, but I suggest using a pair of tweezers. These will insure your getting a good grip and will eliminate the possibility of the tick attaching itself to you. Flea powder can be used to rid your cat of this pest. Flea and tick powder are available separately or in a combined form.

MAGGOTS can also be a problem, particularly in a cat that is not well, not kept clean or that has a sore that is healing. Flies are attracted to the sore, or even to the cat's hind end if he has been having the runs. If the fly lays eggs, they will hatch into maggots, which eat into the cat's skin. They result in a very sick cat. Flea powder may control it temporarily, but a vet is necessary to find the exact spots where the maggots are and get them out without harm to the cat. Keeping your cat clean at all times and treating open sores is the safest way to stay out of trouble. If flies find their way into the house, get rid of them. Outdoor cats are a bigger problem; keep an eye out for trouble.

INSECTS can cause trouble as their bites will result in swelling (an allergic reaction). The best treament for common swelling is an antiallergenic which fights the swelling, itching, and irritation. Bites come from ants, spiders, mosquitoes, and bees (the latter, if on the tongue or mouth, may be fatal).

MITES are another problem. Though not visible to the human eye, a brownish wax in the ears usually signals their presence. They will cause irritation to the ear and misery for the cat. They can be spread from one cat to another, but never to people. As with fleas, mites must be killed as adults. There are many preparations specifically for cats and ear mites. Sometimes you can clean the ear out yourself with Q-tips and mineral oil, being careful not to dig too deep or irritate any inflammation caused by the mites. A vet can be called in to clean out the ear all the way into the middle ear, where mites may have traveled.

Another type of mite causes what is known as SARCOPTIC

MANGE. The mite gets into the skin. It usually begins at the head, but may start at any point on the body with the mite burrowing into the skin, sweat glands or hair follicles. It starts as small red patches that turn into liquid-filled swellings. These open and discharge a fluid that forms scabs. The result is shedding and itching. This condition is transmittable to people. The area should be cleansed and medication specifically intended for the mange should be applied.

Another type of mite causes what is known as the RED MANGE. In this case, again, the mites get into the glands of the cat's skin and hair follicles. It results in hairless areas where the mite strikes. At first the spots are red in color, thus the name. Then the hairless spots enlarge and irritation and itching occur. Treatment should be the same as for other mite conditions.

The last parasites to be discussed are LICE. These parasites also bite and suck blood. They will lay their eggs on the skin and fur of the cat. Watch for them particularly in kittens where they can cause anemia. Flea powder is also effective on these pests.

In addition to these external parasites, there is one type of parasite that attacks the cats internally. The internal protozoan parasite is Coccidia which results in COCCIDIOSIS and attacks the small intestine. This is most common in kittens. The animal may have soft, bloody or greyish stools which can contain mucous and will have a foul, distinctive odor. The parasites can usually be found in the feces of the cat by miscroscopic examination. A good, nourishing diet may help the cat afflicted with this condition. However, cleanliness is a must as the condition is persistent and highly transmittable. Vet care is necessary, for if not cured the cat will become a carrier infecting other cats.

Worms

There are two common varieties of worms your cat can acquire. One is the ROUNDWORM. These worms occur in-

ternally and can be found in the cat's stools or may be
passed off by the cat in vomiting. They are visible to the
naked eye, are white and look like a thin earthworm. The
worms wander through the bloodstream from the intestinal
wall where they hatch. They invade all the vital organs.
They sap the cat's strength, dull his coat, ruin his appetite.
The worms can be passed on to unborn kittens who are then
born with roundworms and may die of them. The worm is
easily picked up by one cat when passed off by another. They
lodge on the cat's paw and are licked off and taken into
the cat's system. Roundworms are usually removed by
medication, but this should be done under the supervision
of a vet. As with parasites, the adult worm is the one that
is vulnerable to medication. Often treatment must be repeated.

TAPEWORMS constitute a second worm problem of cats.
These worms or pieces of them are passed off in the stool
and can be seen there or sticking to the fur around the anus.
Again, a vet is necessary. There is medication that can help
to dislodge and destroy the heads of the worms, which are
lodged in the intestinal walls. Usually cats can get tapeworm
from eating a flea which has eaten a passed-off tapeworm
egg. Repeated treatments are often necessary.

Hairballs

These occur when the cats swallow loose hair that comes
off as they clean themselves. If too many hairs are swallowed
they ball up and are vomited. Often this will gag the cat.
They can also be passed out of the rectum. A good way to
aid the passing of such hairballs is by using any oil or
other lubricant not harmful to cats (olive oil, for example).
Give this by spoon, eyedropper, or by smearing it on the
cat's paw to be licked off and into the body. Good grooming of your cat can cut down on this problem. Grooming
will eliminate dead hairs before the cat can lick them off
and swallow them.

Diarrhea

This is another minor problem. It can be caused by eating the wrong foods, which cause digestive trouble. This can be treated with Kaopectate (it is not harmful to the cat) or with boiled milk or cottage cheese given every few hours. It is well at this time to avoid unboiled milk and even eggs which seldom cause this problem on their own, but can contribute to the condition if it already exists. If the problem persists and is combined with other symptoms, such as fever, indicative of a sick cat, stomach disorder, viruses, infection, and even intestinal blockage may be suspected. You may even suspect changes in diet or ordinary problems like worms.

Constipation

This can be caused by hairballs, which block the intestines. If this is the cause, treat accordingly. It also may be due to a faulty diet, in which case a choice of food that is laxative in effect is advised. Liver, milk, horsemeat or even olive oil will serve the purpose. If no movements or constipation with vomiting occurs, obstruction of some kind may be indicated. See your vet immediately.

Poisoning

This is often contracted by outdoor cats who get into poison that has been set out for mice or rats. They also are susceptible to poisoning by chewing the leaves of plants and bushes that have been sprayed with insecticides. Even brushing against plants treated with such chemicals can poison the cat when he washes himself and thus introduces the poison into his system. Inside you must take precautions not to spray your plants with insecticides, not to allow your cat access to chemicals, medications, actual poisons, and deodorizers, and to keep household plants out of the reach of cats. Aside from chemicals sprayed on the plants, the plants themselves may be harmful—even poisonous. Cats seem to enjoy munching plants; do not allow this. Plant poison causes symptoms such as irritation of the mucous membranes, vomiting, diarrhea, listlessness, liver and kidney trouble, salivation and renal failure or neurological disturbances. Philodendron, if eaten, is poisonous. Ivy too is poisonous. Poinsettia leaves and stems cause gastroenteritis. Rhododendron causes salivation, nasal and tear discharge, vomiting, convulsions, paralysis and death. Mistletoe causes vomiting, diarrhea, slow pulse and affects the heart if any part, especially the berries, is eaten. If you think your cat has been poisoned, try to induce vomiting with dishwater, soap, or hydrogen peroxide and water. Take him immediately to the vet. The universal antidote should be remembered in poisoning cases: burned toast (charcoal), two parts; milk of magnesia, one part; tea, one part. If you want to keep both your plants and cats, keep your plants out of the cat's reach.

Liver Trouble

This may be a temporary problem showing up in greyish, smelly stools. It is usually caused by improper digestion of fat. The fur may look and feel greasy and the skin may be oily. The cat will look sick, listless and may get thin. Usually the problem is one of faulty metabolism, an imbalance that is temporary. If, however, the trouble persists, a vet should check for real damage to the liver.

Anemia

This may be simple anemia, caused by a lack of hemoglobin (red blood cells). The gums, tongue, nose and nails will become pale and the area around the eyes may be pale too. In this case iron is necessary for the cat and liver is one good source of this. Iron tonic, B-complex and B-12 vitamins can also be given beneficially. Watch for this condition in pregnant and nursing females. A more severe type of anemia is called Feline Infectious Anemia and is usually transmitted by fleas. The carrier flea will bite the cat, who will become sick. Other fleas that bite this cat will, upon biting a healthy one, transmit the condition further. Treat the cat and get rid of the fleas. The situation can cause loss of blood, which might require so drastic a remedy as a blood transfusion. Signs of real trouble are fever, depression, emaciation, loss of appetite and jaundice. Antibiotics are then useful.

Cystitis

This is an inflammation of the bladder that can lead to urinary or bladder stones. The bladder is usually located in the back of the abdominal cavity; when it is distended it can be felt at the front of the abdomen. This distended bladder is a symptom of cystitis. Other symptoms include sudden bad bladder habits, vomiting, a large abdomen, a urine odor to the breath, depression, pain on urinating, dehydration, difficulty in passing urine, bloody urine, and straining when trying to urinate.

Causes of this condition include eating too much cat food with a high ash content (3.5 should be the maximum in canned cat food), urine retention (which causes urinary salts to collect as crystals); not enough water intake; a lack of vitamin A, which causes the bladder wall to be less resistant; food poor in vitamins, causing low resistance; stress, which weakens the body and leaves it open to colds; direct trauma to the bladder because of injury; too little exercise; and castration, which may cause less urination.

It is a common disorder of mature cats and more common to tom or altered cats. A vet should be called to treat the condition. This condition can get worse and develop into two other conditions, bladder stones and uremic poisoning. The latter will cause this poison to go through the whole system, resulting in death in a short period of time. The case of bladder stones is a little different. For the smaller ones, a medication can be used to dissolve the stones.

Surgery is necessary for larger ones. These stones are like grains of sand (actually salt) which pack together and lodge in the urethral passage. For this condition a lower than usual diet of ash is recommended. Vitamin A is also an aid in avoiding a recurrence. Avoid canned food with high calcium and ash content, which they all have regardless of their advertisements. Fluid therapy, force feeding and vitamins are essential in advanced cases. Antibiotics are available, as well as sulfa drugs which have been successful in treating the problem. Always turn to your vet; do not administer drugs by yourself. You are not qualified to decide the type or the dosage of drugs your cat needs.

Swelling, Tumors, and Abscesses

Swelling usually indicates an injury or infection. Infection internally must be treated with antibiotics. Externally, the swollen area can be lanced to let out the poisons. Keeping the area clear and clean until the infection is healed is important. Tumors are not common to animals, but do occur occasionally. If a swelling grows, it should be checked by a vet; it might be a tumor. If it is he will do a biopsy. The tumor must be surgically removed by a vet. Abscesses are a common feline problem. This occurs mostly in those cats who roam freely and get into fights. They receive injuries, which in turn do not heal properly. The cat will be tender in the area of injury and may lose his appetite and become listless. Small scabs will develop where the abscess is located and the area will swell up. This will require treatment by a vet if the cat is not to lose much tissue due to damage. The longer the condition goes on, the more tissue damage is done.

Ear Troubles

In addition to such troubles as ear mites there is also the problem of bloody tumors. When an injury to the ear causes broken blood vessels, blood goes into the tissues. This type of damage can occur if your cat scratches at ear mites. Again, a vet should treat the trouble. Medication is available for these and other ear troubles. Be sure, though, to check with the vet, and when treating the condition yourself, go gently as the ear is a delicate, easily injured area.

Eye Troubles

One eye problem can be the oozing of pus from the eye. This can be an indication of disease, but if so it is usually accompanied by other symptoms. It can also be caused by a scratch in the eye that results in irritation. For the normal, runny eye, there is a product that will eliminate the problem. There are also products that can remove eye stain from where the eye has run. Many things can cause eye inflammation, including dust, dirt, fumes and even cat hair floating in the eye. There are ointments and lotions to help inflammation and solutions for cleaning out the eye. Boric acid is a good solution for this purpose. You can tell an irritation by the redness around the inside of the eyelid, discharge, and pus. Ulcers are also common and should be treated by a vet. When using cotton to clean the affected eye, be sure not to touch the good eye with the same cotton swab. This will quickly transfer the problem to the good eye. A good way to cleanse the eye is to soak the cotton in the solution and squeeze it into the eye. The cat will automatically blink and thus distribute the solution throughout the eye. When using an ointment, put a dab in and rub the eye when it is closed to distribute the ointment throughout the eye.

Cataracts may occur in a cat. They appear as a white film and eventually will cause the loss of sight in the affected eye. Surgery can be done, but is not always successful. Damage to the eye can occur in birth or by accident. In the first case, a kitten can be born with one or both eyes open. They will then close and you may not realize that damage has been done. In a month or more the eye will develop a white film and will appear dead. Naturally, this makes the cat un-showable. It can also affect the cat's vision. Damage by young children or another cat is also an unfortunate case of damage. A hard-enough poke in the eye will damage it internally and you will see the results in a white film inside the eye. Again, the cat is not showable and again eyesight can be affected. To avoid this unnecessary situation, keep young children and their curious fingers away from the kitten and keep the claws of other kittens cut.

Skin Troubles

RINGWORM: Contrary to its name, this condition is not caused by a worm. Rather, it is a fungus disease. The problem usually starts on the head, and may spread to the face, legs, or other parts of the cat. The area affected can be any shape, but is usually round and is always hairless. If not treated by a vet, who will determine what type of fungus has caused the condition (or if it is instead an allergic reaction), it can spread and the area of the lesion will get larger and form crusty pinkish patches, which are raised and darker pink around the edge. Scratching is a natural reaction. To treat ringworm, clip the hair away from the affected area. Be careful not to touch it yourself, as the condition is transmittable to people. Scrape off the scab, and apply iodine, iodine salve, or another ringworm preparation. A vet can be called in for treatment if the problem persists.

DANDRUFF: Another skin condition that will cause your cat discomfort. These are white scales or flakes of skin on the cat's fur. They are usually greyish and have a dirty appearance. It is caused by a fat-secretion imbalance, a thyroid disturbance, or some parasites inside the animal. It can also be caused by a faulty diet, or it can be an indication of a disease somewhere in the system of the cat. A vet should check the cat for a more serious condition. Dandruff itself should be treated with medication for that particular problem.

ECZEMA: A fairly common condition among cats. There

are many causes: fleas, irritation from medications used to deflea cats, or a vitamin deficiency due to faulty diet. Symptoms are itching, loss of hair, dandruff, discharge, and scabs. The area affected is the base of the tail, shoulders, behind the ears, neck, scrotum, and vulva. A vet should determine if it is indeed eczema, in which case treatment can be started. Anti-allergenic shots, bathing the areas with a medicated shampoo, or an ointment specifically designed for eczema are all useful treatments. It is good to keep the area affected free of fur to aid the treatment.

Mouth Disorder

TARTAR on the teeth can make your cat's mouth sore and cut down on his appetite. Tartar, made up of calcium salts, bacteria and food, tends to accumulate on the teeth and irritates the gums, eventually causing an infection. If the tartar is not removed and infection does set in, it can spread throughout the whole system, localizing in the heart, kidneys and other organs.

TEETHING is a problem with kittens between four and seven months old. At this time they loose their baby teeth and cut permanent teeth. The mouth will be sore and the kitten may not want to eat, or may start to eat and give up due to pain. Help can be given in the form of liquid or mashed food. His gums may also be sore and drooling may occur. He may even have upset bowels and a temperature. This is all natural, but if a tooth seems to cause persistent trouble, consult a vet.

GINGIVITIS occurs when too much tartar accumulates on the teeth. Symptoms include red, swollen gums, drooling, and a reluctance to eat. A vet can remove the tartar, which may spread under the gums. He may have to treat the gums with antibiotics if infection has set in. You can help by washing your cat's mouth out with a salt and water solution. To avoid tartar accumulation in the first place, give your cat chunks of meat to chew or small quantities of dried cat food.

These both exercise the gums and cut down on tartar. Be
sure dead or loose teeth are removed before they irritate
and infect the gums.

SWALLOWING FOREIGN OBJECTS is a minor problem. A
cat can pick up anything small and accidentally swallow it.
A pin, needle, tack (from furniture), pieces of cloth, string,
or any other small object can attract the cat's attention, and
taken into the mouth can be swallowed. You can help by
removing the piece if you can find where it has lodged in
the throat. If you are not successful, or if the object has
gone too far down, go immediately to your vet. The cat will
let you know immediately when he has swallowed an object:
he will panic, choke, drool, paw at his mouth, and hold his
mouth open, struggling for breath.

MAJOR PROBLEMS

Rabies

This severe condition is usually transmitted to cats from
most any other mammal. There is no vaccination against it,
as it is rare except in epidemic situations. It is transmitted
through the saliva of an infected animal, when the infected
animal bites a healthy one. The incubation period is usually
ten days. Symptoms include a sudden change in the cat's behavior. Usually the cat becomes more wild, restless, fearful,
antagonistic; or he can become a recluse. The voice may
change, becoming hoarse and low. Drooling occurs. Later
appetite is lost, drinking and swallowing become difficult,
bowel movement is harder, and there may be convulsions.
The duration is short, and usually the disease is fatal. If
you think your cat has become infected, turn him over to a
vet. If you or someone else has been bitten, immediately
go to your doctor. There are anti-rabies shots available that
are usually effective if given in time. Report this incident
to the health authorities. It is important for them to know,
particularly if you have no way of knowing if your cat may

have bitten someone. They will also want to track down the
animal or animals spreading the problem.

Feline Enteritis
This is commonly known as distemper and is very easily
spread and kills quickly usually 90 percent of the time. There
is an excellent vaccination against this disease, which is
caused by a virus that is airborne and is transmitted through
the air. Young cats are more susceptible to this disease, although a cat of any age can get it. After the initial vaccination shots, booster shots should be given each year. If the
animal has come in contact with one already afflicted, shots
should be given immediately. Being airborne, the virus can
be aloft in an area where a sick cat has been. The incubation period between the time of exposure and when the first
symptoms appear is four to seven days. The symptoms are
a loss of appetite, attempting to drink water (but the cat will
just sit with his head over the dish), a tail that gets very
thin, fur that becomes dull and stands on end, listlessness, a
lack of energy, slovenliness, diarrhea, vomiting yellow
liquid, weakness, and a high fever. Dehydration sets in and
the cat becomes emaciated and will soon die. In kittens it
can kill quickly. Cats often appear to be getting better only
to worsen or die suddenly. In older cats they may drag on
(literally) for a week or more.
If your cat does get distemper, take him to a vet. The
vet will introduce fluids to counteract dehydration and will
administer antibiotics. If you keep the animal at home, keep
the temperature in the home constant, make him comfortable, and be sure and keep fluids going into the cat. Again,
boiled milk, Pepto-Bismol or Kaopectate can control diarrhea, which in itself can be dehydrating. Groom the cat
daily, as he probably will not do it himself. This will also
make him feel a little better. It is best, though, to let a vet
handle the situation.

Pneumonitis

This is not to be confused with Pneumonia. It is a cat's disease and affects the respiratory system. It is caused by a virus. This condition is not usually fatal if treatment is given and if the cat is in good condition to begin with. The symptoms are runny eyes and nose, a sore throat, sneezing fits, coughing, listlessness, slight fever, loss of appetite, loss of weight and loose bowels. When you find your cat has this condition, isolate him from other cats in the house. Also isolate those cats with whom he has been in contact. The disease can be transmitted through the air or on objects that the cat has been near. A vet should see the cat to discover if the animal does indeed have pneumonitis and not another respiratory virus (of which there are many). This condition needs immediate treatment, as it will go through the whole respiratory tract from eyes, nose, throat, and even intestines. Finally it will enter the lungs, making breathing difficult. The cat will be weak, especially if he cannot eat. Antibiotics will be used by the vet and force feeding can be carried out. Light feeding can also be beneficial. Good nursing, keeping a constant temperature and a food that will give nourishment and not cause diarrhea is important. There are vaccinations for this, but vets are finding that there are so many strains of this disease that one shot may not avoid getting another strain of the disease. A shot will, however, cut down on the severity if the disease does strike (whatever strain it is). Shots should be given regularly as they wear off rapidly. If you are going to a show, this is a must to avoid or cut down on a condition your cat may contract there.

Rhinotracheitis

This condition is known as "Rhino" in the cat world. It is similar to the flu in people, but is much more dangerous in cats. It is fatal to kittens who are born with it (having gotten it probably from their mothers). The condition resembles Pneumonitis. The duration of the condition is long, and response to medication is poor and slow. There are recurring eye infections and frequent relapses. Females carry this virus in their system. It is triggered again when the mother cat has given birth to her kittens. Then, she and the kittens come down with it again. The most obvious sign is constant sneezing. Much research is still going on about this condition.

NURSING A SICK CAT

Medicating

Giving a pill to a cat may very likely require the combined efforts of two people: one to hold the cat, the other actually to give the pill. The following procedure is for right handed people; if you are left handed just reverse it.

To give a pill place your left hand over the cat's head and put your thumb under the right side of his chin and the first two fingers of your hand under the left side of his chin. With your little finger put pressure on his neck to hold him steady. Then with your right hand take the pill between your thumb and your index finger. With your left hand hold the cat's head back firmly, then with your middle finger of the right hand pry open the mouth. Using the left hand quickly tilt the head back as you move the mouth open wider with your middle finger of the right hand. By now your cat's mouth should be open and his head should be steady. Place the pill, which you are holding in your right hand between index finger and thumb, as far back in the cat's mouth as possible and quickly close the mouth. To induce swallowing wet the cat's mouth with your finger and hold him until he swallows or massage the cat's throat.

If this method does not work with your cat (some are very stubborn about taking pills) you can resort to a few tricks. You can mash up the pill and put it in a favorite food. You can also mash it up with liquid and put it into a syringe and feed it as you would liquid medication, but use the plunger on the syringe to force the fluid into the cat's mouth. In giving liquid medication, hold the cat in the same manner. Give the liquid by syringe, spoon, or eye dropper. Be sure to give it slowly so that the cat will not choke by swallowing too fast or getting too much at once.

SUPPLIES AND EQUIPMENT
TO HAVE ON HAND

Rectal Thermometer
Flea and Tick Powder
Sulfa Drugs
Antibiotics
Ear Mite Medication
Mange Medication
Skin and Coat Conditionsrs
Tweezers
Cotton Balls
A Spoon
Ear Drops
Canker Powder or Drops (Ear)
Ear Ointment
Gauze

Eye Stain Inhibitor
Eye Stain Remover
Eye Wash
Eye Ointment
Boric Acid Ointment or Solution
Anti-Itch Solutions or Shampoos
Ointment, Tablets, Solutions for
    Skin Conditions
Iodine and Iodine Salve
Eczema Shampoo and Ointment
Blankets
Eye Dropper
Vaseline
Adhesive Tape

4

What You Always Wanted to Know About Sex ... and Cats

THE MALE

Reproductive Organs

The male is distinguished by his testicles, which are suspended outside the body cavity. It is here that the sperm are manufactured. The scrotum is a sack or pouch that supports the testicles. The penis is the organ which makes a male a male, and which is inserted into the female cat's vagina and through which the sperm enter the vagina for breeding.

Behavior

The normal mature male will usually be anxious to find a female—whether she is willing or not. He has no particular "girl" in mind and will try to mate with even a kitten or a pregnant cat even though it is obvious that they are not in heat. He may even go after another male to satisfy his stud urge. Mating is foremost in his mind: before eating, before his master's affection, before play. If he is caged he will want out; if he is an outdoor cat he will prowl and howl until you let him out. You may have problems with a cat you let roam, as he may battle other cats for a female or may roam from home to find his favorite "lady friend."

In the process, he may get bitten, clawed, or mauled. He may even get lost. If you do not let him out to fulfill his male needs he may wet or spray. (The cat's way of staking out his territory.) This is his way of showing he is a male. Some, if you are lucky, will not spray; but this is up to the individual cat and has nothing to do with his potency.

Neutering or Castrating

Whichever term you choose to use, you eliminate the male's urge to be male. It is best done at five or six months of age, particularly in those not highly bred, who will come into maturity much earlier than their more aristocratic counterparts. Neutering is simply done by a vet. An anesthetic is used, of course. It will probably mean a night's stay at the vet and should cost about ten dollars. By doing this simple thing (if you do not intend to breed your male) you will eliminate his mating urge. He will then no longer roam, his urine will not get that unmistakable odor, he will not spray, nor will he annoy your neighbors with constant howling. Just remember that neutered males are more prone to urinary stones and so avoid diets high in ash and calcium.

Problems of the Male

One problem is monorchidism. This is the case of a male who has only one testicle that can be seen. If one testicle does not drop in its position in the scrotum, then the cat will only be half as fertile. The reason is that if the testicle is up inside the body the body temperature is detrimental to the sperm. This can be an inherited trait and therefore it is unwise to breed your monorchid cat or breed with one that is. In neutering this type of cat the procedure is more complicated. The testicle that remains "inside" must be found and put out of commission, because otherwise the male will still have the same male urges, though procreation will not occur. Cryptorchism is a second problem. Here, neither testicles have descended to the scrotum from the body cavity. The male urge is intact, but the cat is sterile. Both testicles must be removed to eliminate the mating urge. Another problem is lack of fertility. If this occurs, hormone injections are helpful to make the sperm more numerous or give those present more power. They can also be used to increase the male's desire if you have babied him into forgetting his male urges or if he was born not caring about mating.

THE FEMALE

Reproductive Organs

There are two ovaries located inside the body cavity. It is here that the eggs or ova are produced. The ovaries are similar to the testicles in the male. The uterus is a "Y"-shaped organ and it is here that the kittens will live until birth. Fallopian tubes connect the ovaries to the uterus and are the organs through which pass the eggs. The cervix is where the uterus terminates, and the vagina begins. The vagina is the outside area of the reproduction tract and it is where the male cat places the penis and deposits the sperm. The vulva consists of the external parts of the reproductive organs.

Behavior of the Female and Breeding

The female, unlike the male, is only in season or "in heat" on occasions, depending on the individual cat. The first heat occurs in different cats at the time of that cat's maturity, whether it be six months (common for domestic cats) or two years (as sometimes happens in highly bred females). The frequency of periods of heat varies in individual cats. Some authorities believe it depends on heredity. They think mothers and their female offspring are similar in their sexual patterns. When the female comes into "heat" she will let you know. She may rub against anything she can find, she may become talkative, she may even give little love calls. The female will become particularly demonstrative if a male is near, luring him into breeding. She will meow, roll around, eat more, raise her rump in the air (particularly if you rub her at the base of her tail), slink down and wiggle her hind end on the ground in a rubbing manner. You can be certain she is in heat if you pat her behind and her tail goes immediately to one side. As she gets ready to accept the male her crying will be louder and her antics more pronounced. Some females may even spray or wet. When they do mate they will be loud, and most females yell when they are taken.

Courtships are short and loud. The male will mount the female, grasping her by the back of the neck (leaving telltale breeding marks) and forcing her into the desired position. The cries will usually occur when the penis is inserted. The heat season of a cat will come and go, and unless the cat is bred, heat will recur until she is. Most females come into heat in late winter, spring and early summer. Even nursing cats can come into heat again. It is not good to breed too often, as this will weaken the female, especially if she is highly bred. Her looks will deteriorate and she will not be so happy or healthy. Allow her time between litters to recuperate physically. There are drugs which can be purchased that make the female scent unknown to the male and discourage mating. If you wish to breed your cat, here is some advice that will help. If your male is young, breed him with a proven, experienced female as she will give him assurance and cooperation. Similarly, if your female is young use a proven, experienced male or she may get away from him altogether because of her fear of the new situation.

Spaying

If you do not wish to breed your female and you do not wish her going through needless heats without satisfaction (not to mention the suitors who will noisily call), then spaying is the only answer. If you never intend to breed her, spay at an early age, between six and eight months. If your cat has had kittens wait until she is finished nursing and has dried up. When the operation is done (by a vet) the entire reproductive system of the female is removed. An incision is made and the organs are removed. You will receive her back with a temporary bandage around her middle. The cost is higher than for a male, usually about twenty to twenty-five dollars, because it is more extensive surgery.

EFFECTS OF ALTERING IN MALES AND FEMALES

We have already discussed the fact that spaying or castrating will rid the cat of the sex urge . . . if the operation was done properly and was complete. They will have time for other things and may be more affectionate and playful. Longhairs will tend to hold their fur better due to the fact that there is no mating season for them any longer. Your cat will also fill out more and may become calmer. You can still show these altered cats but in their own categories. This will be explained later in the book.

PREGNANCY

Symptoms
It takes a while for a cat to show symptoms; this usually occurs around the fourth week. Then the nipples may become darker, brighter pink, and enlarge. Some expectant cats do not show this change in nipples until the end of the gestation period. The cat will become fuller. A vet can tell at about three weeks. Your cat may become more hungry, may lie around and become lazy, or go hunting into nooks for a place to nest. If there is newspaper around, they may shred it up in an attempt to make a nest. Some cats become cross, others more affectionate. In the early stages, vomiting may occur. In the last few weeks loose bowels are common.

It is good for your cat to see the vet for a check-up and you should also check for conditions that may be passed on to the kittens. This means checking stools for worms, the skin for any skin condition or parasite. Be sure the cat is eating well. The number of meals may be increased as your cat's appetite will increase. Vitamins should be faithfully given. At five or six weeks the kittens may be noticed, even felt, as small balls in the mother's stomach. The cat will grow larger and her appetite will continue to increase. Be sure she is getting raw meat, vegetables, milk (if the cat can take it) or cottage cheese, egg yolk, and vitamins. At about eight weeks the breasts will enlarge and there will be milk, causing some soreness to the cat. She may lick her stomach. And either by cleaning her nipples or by their continual enlargement, her hair will grow away from the nipples.

Gestation Period

The period of gestation for a cat is usually nine weeks. An average of 63 days, give or take a day or two on either end, is usual. Sometimes you must guess because you do not know the exact day of breeding if the male and female were together for a few days. If the cat goes over 65 days have her checked by a vet. Also, if delivery starts and more than half a day goes by between kittens, the last kittens will probably be born dead. It has been known to happen that kittens born days apart can still live, but if a kitten seems to be late in arriving after his brothers and sisters it is best to take the mother to a vet. How long your cat will carry may be the same each time, or it may vary. Close observation on your part will tell you whether yours is predictable or predictably unpredictable. You will get to know your cat and her cycles. How many kittens you can expect, too, on the average, may be determinable from previous experience with the cat in question.

Miscarriage or Premature Birth

A cat may miscarry so early that you may know one

minute the cat is pregnant, while the next the pregnancy is gone—with the cat cleaning up the passed off fetus and placenta. Or, you may not notice it at all because the passed off fetus is so small. In later miscarriages there will be labor and a miscarriage you definitely will notice. Some kittens may make it alive, others may not. A cat that constantly miscarries is not capable of carrying and should be spayed for her comfort and your peace of mind. Causes of miscarriage may vary: some may not carry because the fetus is imperfect and it is nature's way to remove a cat that is not meant to be born; some females cannot carry full term at all; some have trouble within the uterus or in its shape or size; sickness may be a factor and injury may be a cause. If your cat does miscarry, try again; however, have her checked by a vet for innate problems. If she does not carry the second time, have her spayed. Premature kits do not usually live more than a day or two. They are not ready for the world and even with care they are just not strong enough or mature enough to survive. Never blame yourself for what nature decides is best.

BIRTH

This is a wonder to behold—no matter how many times you view it. Experienced females may leave you free to watch in wonder while they handle it all instinctively. At first, you will notice certain behavior patterns: the cat may stop eating, look for a place to nest, won't leave your side, and eventually go into labor. You can help her by being there, particularly if it is her first time. Prepare her by cutting the hair away from the delivery area and the nipples (if necessary). Be careful in this procedure, especially around the enlarged, sensitive nipples. If there has been a slight flow from the nipples, clean them off with cotton and oil. Your cat will decide where she wants to have her kittens. Perhaps you will prefer her in a different place, like a cage. The latter is best if your cat is not the only one in the house. Jealous females and curious (and jealous) males may annoy the mother cat and later bother the kittens. In a cage you will know where to find the kittens and they will be safe. The mother, of course, will protect them wherever they are born. If it is not to be a cage, the cat may appreciate a box with a hole cut in it. She can make her nest there quite happily. Wherever you and the cat decide on, set up a comfortable nest using receiving blankets to keep the cat warm and clean (newspapers are popular, but they are anything but clean). When the cat seems ready to settle into her nest you must just wait with her for the new arrivals. Let the cat do all she can. Be sure, though, that each kit is delivered fully and that the mother breaks the sac and cleans off the face fully so the kitten can breathe. Also be sure the kitten finds its way to a nipple to nurse. If the mother has trouble delivering, you can help her. If she delivers too fast and cannot get to a kitten right away or is too inexperienced or lazy to take care of them as they are born, you must do the job she should do. Watch for kittens that are born and get lost in the shuffle. When a kitten is born and the mother does not take care of it, open the sac yourself, clean the face and the nose area especially and be sure the kitten is breathing. If the kitten does not, check the nose again and shake the kitten gently (holding the head firmly) to force air into its nose. When it is breathing on its own, find it a nipple and watch for others to help. If the mother does not cut the cord herself, you must do this too. Use a blunt scissor. Also be sure that after a birth the placenta is also passed off. If it is left inside the cat, infection will follow. The placenta, by nature, will be eaten by the mother. This is nature's nourishment for the mother. Cats are basically instinctive and clean in their habits and in the birthing of their kittens. Be sure new kittens are not stepped on accidentally by the mother or sat on or left without a nipple to nurse from. The mother cat will, though it may amaze you, purr through the whole process. After delivery feed the

mother well and when she is free to leave the kittens awhile
have her checked by a vet to cover any latent infections or
problems left over from the pregnancy or delivery.

KITTENS

The kittens will live where they are born. The mother
will probably venture out after they are fed and visit with
her human family. She may want to eat away from the kittens. Every mother needs a rest! The kittens at first cannot
see or hear and they crawl around because their legs are too
weak to hold them. Keep children away from the kittens.
Do not handle them yourself either in this early stage.
Leave them in peace and quiet. They will be busy finding
nipples and nursing. Be sure they all get enough to eat.
Also be sure they are kept warm. Don't allow the largest of
the litter to hog the snack bar. A bad mother should be
prompted to fulfill her obligations. If the mother cannot
provide enough milk, you can help out. Use a half-and-half
mixture of evaporated milk and water, plus some vitamin
supplement. Use an eye dropper and feed about every three
to four hours or five or six times a day. Be sure the for-
mula is slightly warmed. The kittens should feel firm and
their skin should be resilient. A kitten should not look thin,
weak, or be crying all the time. The latter is a sign of
hunger.

Weaning
Around the third, fourth, or fifth week—depending on
the size of the kitten—weaning should begin. The mother
cat will do this, too; she will begin to spend less time with
the kittens. Start with baby cereal. Add strained baby meat
and vegetables. Egg yolk and cottage cheese can be used
profitably. As the kitten grows add raw meat and serve all
these at room temperature. Complete weaning should be
over at eight weeks and the kittens should be on the regular

diet of your older cats.

The mother will train the kittens and play with them and teach them their toilet habits. Now is the time to get your kittens ready for the world outside their mother and their litter mates. Handle them gently, groom them a little to get them used to being handled. Play with them, yet teach them gentleness. Immunization transmitted to the kitten from the mother will wear off approximately two weeks after weaning. Eight weeks is recommended for distemper for vaccinations. Usually temporary shots are given, each ten days apart.

SUPPLIES AND EQUIPMENT
TO HAVE ON HAND

Baby Oil
Blankets
Anti-Mating Spray
Cage Drapes
Scissors
Cotton Balls

Baby Cereal
Baby Egg Yolks
Baby Meats
Vitamin Supplements
Eye Dropper
Evaporated Milk

5

Presenting the Pedigree

THE PEDIGREE

A cat is considered to be pedigreed if it can trace its parentage back four generations; it is usually bred to better the breed. It has a special name that bears the cattery name where it was bred and the cattery name that bought the cat as a kitten. It is usually registered with one or more associations and has registration papers for each association. It has been bred selectively, purposely; its selling price represents the value of the animal, its breeding, its future stud or breeding value, and its show value. All the breeds described in the first chapter *may* be pedigree cats. Those *not* sold with papers are sold strictly as pets, because they are not considered up to the high standards of the breeder. They are still pedigrees, but they do not have the papers enabling them to carry on their branch of the pedigree line. Below is a sample and explanation of a pedigree—an exceptionally fine one.

Notice that the association's name is on the top of an official pedigree. When a cat is registered by his breeder, the breeder is given a choice of two names. This is because no two cats registered with an association may have the same name. The blank box is where the breeder will place the registration number of the cat whose pedigree this is. No-

NAME Quad. Ch. Fergus's Shelley Boy of Theta   Reg. No.

Breed Persian   Color Shell Cameo   Eye Color Copper   Sex Male   Born 12/6/70

Owner Mr. and Mrs. Robert H. Wilson   Address 8 Vancouver Avenue, Warwick, R.I. 02886

PARENTS	GRAND PARENTS	GREAT GRAND PARENTS
SIRE Gr. + Ch. Fergus's Honey Bear II	RM Quad. Ch. Montpellier Royal Noel	Gr. + Ch. Montpellier Royalty of Lone Pine
No.	No.	No.
Breed Persian	Color C.B. White	Color C.B. White
Color Shell Cameo		Gr. + Gr. Ch. Montpellier Chanteuse
Owner Mr. and Mrs. A.D. Fergus	RM Quad. Ch. Fergus's Pink Taffy of Lekarm	No.
Address P.O. Box 571	No.	Color Shell Cameo
Sutherline, Oregon 97479	Color Shell Cameo	RM Gr. Ch. Fergus's Honey Bear of Flower Lane
		No.
		Color Shell Cameo
		Chatami Mtaine of Fergus's
		No.
		Color
DAM Fergus's Tonala	Gr. + Ch. Fergus's Honey Bear II	Silver Cameo Tortie
No.	No.	No.
Breed Persian	Color Shell Cameo	Color
Color Cameo Tortie		RM Quad. Ch. Montpellier Royal Noel
Owner Mr. and Mrs. A.D. Fergus	RM Dbl. Ch. + Ch. Fergus's Tiny Satin Doll	No.
Address P.O. Box 571	No.	Color C.B. White
Sutherline, Oregon 97479	Color Blue-Cream	RM Quad. Ch. Fergus's Pink Taffy of Lekarm
		No.
		Color Shell Cameo
		RM Gr. + Gr. Ch. Fergus's Tuck of Coral Gables
		No.
		Color Cream
		Fergus's Tia Maria of Rio Vista
		No.
		Color Blue-Cream

CAT FANCIERS' ASSOCIATION, INC.

I certify that, to the best of my knowledge and belief, the above pedigree is true and correct.

Signed _____

tice that the breed, sex, color, eye color, and birthdate are given for the cat. In addition the owners (sometimes the breeder himself) or new owner's name and address are given. The cattery where the cat was bred and its registration number (if it is registered with the particular association) is also given.

The remainder of the pedigree looks like a family tree. First are given the Sire (the male) and Dam (the female) of the cat. Their registration numbers are given, their breed and color, the owner and the owner's address. The first-generation information is very complete, but as we go back to the second and third generation the only information given is the name of the sire and dam, their color and registration number. Notice, too, that the cat's official titles are given for each feline. Following is a list of abbreviations used in the pedigree:

Ch.—Champion

Gr. Ch.—Grand Champion

Quad. Ch.—A champion in four different associations or in one association that allows a cat to earn more than one championship before going on to his grand championship.

RM—Royal Merit (see Glossary).

Some of these fine cats are grand champions in one association and a champion in another. All their titles are included on the pedigree. In Chapter 6 we will discuss what these cats must do to earn such high titles.

Registering a Pedigree Litter

With pedigree cats you will want to register your litter with one or more associations. You will choose associations that you find sponsor shows in your area, and that have clubs active in your area. You may want to join one or more of these clubs and learn from other breeders about cats in general, your breed and other breeds, and enjoy the company of others who enjoy cats as much as you do. So, when your cats are at least two months old and you know for certain what color and sex they are (this takes a little time) you will send to the association or associations for litter registration forms. Your litter will be assigned a number. You will also receive papers to register each individual kitten. The cost for litter registration is about $2.00 or $3.00, and the same for each kitten registration. If you want the kittens to bear your choice of name you might register them yourself, especially if you intend to keep any of the litter. Otherwise, you can give the new owners the registration form, but be sure and put your cattery name at the beginning of each selection of name for the cat to insure that the cat will be registered with your cattery name indicating you as the breeder of the kitten. This, of course, is when you feel the kitten is up to your standard of quality for a breeder, a stud, a show cat, or a combinationn of these. Otherwise, you may sell the kitten as a pet and charge accordingly. Below is a typical example of a pedigree registration and explanation thereof:

THE CAT FANCIERS' ASSOCIATION, INC.
Certificate of Registration

NAME OF CAT: Zig-Lee's Nanny Tanny of Theta   Reg. No.
DESCRIPTION: Seal Point Himalayan Female Born 1/10/71
SIRE: Gr. Ch. Chestercere Chi Chi of Himba-Tab   Reg. No.
DAM: Harobed's Monique of Zig-Lee   Reg. No.
OWNER: Mr. and Mrs. Robert H. Wilson
         8 Vancouver Avenue
         Warwick, R.I. 02886

BREEDER: Mrs. Donald Zigray
DATE: 5/3/71

Notice that the association that is registering the cat is listed at the top of the registration certificate. The name of the cat is given. Here Zig-Lee cattery is the cattery where the cat was bred and Theta cattery is where the cat now lives. Both these catteries must be registered with this association to use their cattery name. The name in between is the cat's registered name. In this case, and this is true for most cat owners, we do not call our cat by her registered name. She is plain *Tanya* to us. A description of the cat is given along with its registration number. The Sire and Dam are given along with their registration number with that association. The owner's address is given in full. The breeder's name is given and the date of registration. In some associations this registration certificate must be held by the owner in order to show the cat; in others they will honor the registration certificate of another recognized association, but you must register with them to claim a championship if your cat wins one at that particular show.

THE CATTERY

If you are raising cats for profit, are breeding at least one female, and consider yourself a breeder of one or more specific breeds, you may want to register as a cattery. You do not need forty cats, with many studs and queens (females) and a dozen litters to qualify. You need only select a name. Then, write to the association or associations you wish to be registered with and request a cattery registration form. The association will allow you two or three choices in names. No two catteries may have the same name. The cost of registration is between $10.00 and $20.00 depending on the association. You are allowed an average of 12 letters for the cattery name. You may choose your own last name, especially if it is not a common one. You may choose something sentimental to you or something connected with your work or hobbies. A combination of the names of those involved in the venture is one idea. Names seeming to fit the breed are often used, such as Oriental names for Siamese catteries. Use your imagination. When you have registered your cattery you may use your cattery name as a prefix before the names of cats of your breeding and you may also add your cattery as a suffix after your cat's name even if it has the prefix of the cattery that bred it. Try and pick a name that is short to allow you enough letters to meet the limit of 27 set by most associations. If you choose a short cattery name, you may give your cat whatever full name you wish. There may be occasions when a cattery name is acceptable in one association, but already used or not acceptable in another. For example, one cattery is Pittman in most associations, but Pitt in one other. Another cattery is Royal Crown in some associations and Imperial Crown in others. Below is an example of a cattery registration. It is self-explanatory.

CFF   CERTIFICATE OF REGISTRATION
                        OF CATTERY NAME
                  CAT FANCIERS' FEDERATION
THIS CERTIFIES that the Name   THETA   No.
has been registered under the Rules of the Cat Fanciers;
Federation as a Cattery Name
by Mr. and Mrs. Robert H. Wilson, 8 Vancouver Avenue, Warwick, R.I.
for   Their   exclusive use in registering pedigrees in this federation.
Date   April 28, 1971
Fee

                              Signed
                                    Recorder of Registrations

BREEDING

When you begin to breed you have certain decisions to make. You may have a female and male of the same breed housed in your own cattery. If you have only the female you will have to find a stud to breed her to when she comes into heat. Take into consideration when choosing this stud what you are trying to accomplish in your breeding program. If you are trying for a better type or color or other characteristic, pick a stud that will help improve your female's own positive qualities. Be sure to see the stud's pedigree. You are going to pay for the service and you want to be sure the stud is what you want for your queen and has been proven (has sired other females). Sometimes there is a formal agreement; other times there is not. Sometimes the stud's owner will want pick of the litter in place of a fee. Even in an informal agreement certain things will be decided. The fee will be arranged ahead of time. The queen will go to where the stud is housed to be bred. You must find out if the particular breeder will allow your cat to be bred more than once, should it not take the first time, for the initial fee. Some breeders will do this, others will not. When the cat has conceived you will be given the stud's pedigree to enable you to fill out the litter and kitten registrations required when the litter is born. When you own a stud you must decide if you will let him breed with other queens, what you will charge, what arrangements you will make. A good stud with a good pedigree line is worth money as a stud, but then you must consider that while you get the money, the owner of the queen gets the kittens and part of your pedigree and breeding. You must make the choice.

There are numerous ways of breeding, below are a few:

INBREEDING: Here cats very closely related are bred together (such as father and daughter or brother and sister). It can increase good qualities, but can cause trouble for those new in breeding.

LINE BREEDING: This is the most common type of breeding, in which cats not closely related, for example cousin to cousin, are mated.

OUTBREEDING: When cats that are unrelated are bred within a pure breed.

CROSSBREEDING: Mating one breed with another to help perfect cross breeding that has brought about the breed in the first place or in an effort to bring about a new breed. Not a job for a novice.

SELLING YOUR KITTENS

There are numerous ways to sell your kittens. You must first decide what your kittens are worth. There are three categories or perhaps four: pet, breeder, show, and show and breeder. You should never sell a pet cat with any papers and your price should be reasonable to the pet market. Your intention should be to find the cat a good home, but not allow it to be shown or continue its pedigree line. For those who wish only a breeder who may not be show quality, but may produce good kittens, the price will go higher. For a show cat the price is higher still, and for a combination show-breeder cat you ask your highest price. The price will depend upon the demand for the particular breed and the area you live in (unless you go outside the area to sell).

Be sure to check the prices of your breed in your area and in the country as a whole. Now, you can put your pet-quality cat in a pet store and perhaps that is easy. But it is not wise to begin this policy. You will get a reputation for breeding only pet quality, for not caring who gets your cat, and for being out only to make money and not improve the breed. It is best to sell these kittens through your contacts or through a newspaper ad. With those you wish to sell as show or breeding cat you would do well to use *Cats,* the classified section of *Cats* magazine. Their prices are reasonable and they reach the cat market as a whole. You can, if you wish, buy box ads and even put in pictures of your best cats as an example of your breeding. In this magazine you can hunt for the showing or breeding stock you may want also. Another good magazine is *Cat Fancy* and will serve the same purpose. Another market place is the cat show, where you can advertise in the show book when you have kittens or a cat for sale. All this will soon get your name known in the cat world—not just as a breeder of pets, but as a breeder of quality cats intended for continuing the pedigree and doing well at show.

Before ending this chapter it is well to mention that a purchase agreement with the new owners may be valuable. It will be a record (always keep a copy for yourself and give one to the new owner) of your sales and your contacts. It is wise to keep in touch with your kittens and their new owners. The price, type of cat (quality-wise) being sold, and special instructions can be included on this agreement. Some good breeders include a special addition when selling their kittens—a pledge from the new owner known as the Pet Pride Promise:

1. I fully realize my responsibility as I accept this kitten called ———— from ———— on ————.
2. I will keep this kitten with me as long as it lives unless extreme circumstances prevent in which I will notify you and help find suitable placement.
3. I will devote a reasonable time for daily companionship with this kitten.
4. I will make proper provision for this kitten in case of any personal extreme emergency.
5. If at any time the kitten is found to be noticably neglected, I shall willingly return it to its original owner. By neglect, we mean having fleas, ear mites, worms, fungus over a period of time longer than necessary to overcome, continued poor health, being ungroomed or having matted fur, being caged without time for exercise, being left alone long periods of time without human attention or companionship.
6. I agree to follow instructions as to its care, its housing, its food, its treatment and its health.
7. I agree to study a good Cat Care Manual and to follow its instructions.
8. I promise to have ———— altered when almost a year old or if previous arrangements have been made with the original owner agree to breed only to a registered cat.
9. I will never allow my kitten to run loose in the street or on other people's property but its freedom shall be controlled and supervised.
10. I will not declaw my cat.

Birthdate of kitten	New Owner
Sire	Address, tel. no., Zip.
Dam	Original owner, address, tel. no., Zip.

6

On Stage: Cat Shows
and Judging

If you are not just breeding your cat, but also are planning
on entering the exciting world of cat shows—welcome! The
first thing you should know is how to go about getting into
a show, or rather getting your cat into the show. First, *Cats*
Magazine will be your guide here, too, as you watch the
show calendar. For months in advance the shows will be
listed. Look for those in your area, decide how far you
wish to travel, which shows you wish to attend, notice which
associations are sponsoring the shows, and decide if you
wish your cat to compete in that association for awards. In
some associations you must have your cat registered if he
is to compete as a cat (usually not true if a kitten or household pet), others will accept a registration in another recognized association. They will, however, expect you to join
their association in order to claim any championship made
at their show. Start early. About two months before the
show, write for an entry form for each cat or kitten you
wish to enter. When you receive it you will learn if you
must join the association in order to enter. If you do, now
is the time to enter. It will cost you $2.00 to $3.00 for each
cat you wish to register and enter in the show. Below is a
list of addresses you will need:

American Cat Fanciers Association
Mrs. Cora Swan
Box 32
Point Lookout, Missouri 65726

American Cat Association
Louise Murray
16318 Lakewood Blvd.
Bellflower, California 90706

National Cat Fanciers Association
Mrs. Frances Kosierowski
8219 Rosemont
Detroit, Michigan 48228

Cat Fanciers' Federation, Inc.
Mrs. Alice Dickens
3485 Linwood Rd.
Cincinnati, Ohio 45226

Independent Cat Federation
Mrs. Carolyn Alig
3512 East Milton St.
Pasadena, California 91107

United Cat Federation, Inc.
Mr. Ed Bowers
1350 Taft
Lemon Grove, California 92045

Cat Fanciers' Association
P. O. Box 430
Red Bank, New Jersey 07701

It is worth your money to send for the rules and standards
for each association.

You will find that you must send in your entry at least
one month before the show date. This is the reason for
writing early. While you wait for your registration to go
through, fill out the entry blank for each cat or kitten you
plan to enter. You will learn from information on the
entry form the location of the show, the size of the cage,

Name: Dbl. Gr. Ch. and Tri. Ch. Minuet
Frosted Sunset of Mer-C
Sire: Ch. Storm Dancer of Araho
Dam: Darker Clown Princess of Minuet
Breeder: Charles Talley
Owner: Dr. and Mrs. Eugene Couture

the cost of entry for each cat, the cost of a double cage, the cost of showing kittens for sale and how many kittens are allowed per cage, plus what percentage, if any, the association takes for a cat or kitten shown and sold at the show. It varies with the association. Some will take commission only on cats, some on kittens also if they are also being shown in the particular show. You will learn that your kitten must be four months old to be shown. A cat must be eight months old to compete in the championship classes.

Be careful when filling out entry blanks. Fill out all the information correctly. If your cat is not registered with the association to whose show you are going, or if the registration is in progress, be sure and be aware of your cat's exact name as it *will* appear on the registration form when you do get it. Should your cat win a championship you will have to join the association to claim it, even if you did not have to join the association to enter the show. However, the associations are clear about one point. The name that appears in the show book (which will be taken directly from your entry blank) must be exactly like that name on the registration blank. So, if you do not have your cat registered and the form in front of you, write your cat's name as you know you will be registering him. This means: do not use your cattery name as a prefix if the association rules do not allow you to. This is usually always the case if your cattery is not registered with that association. Also, do not use it as a suffix for the same reason. Check with the cattery where your cat was purchased to be sure you may legally use their cattery prefix; that is, if they are registered with the association to whose show you are going. All other information on the entry blank should be exact too. If not, you may make your cat a champion only to have the awards voided because you made an error. Be especially careful if your cattery or cat's name is different in different associations.

Send off your entry blank or blanks with your registration number or numbers (or tell them if your registration is still in progress), and a check covering all costs including advertising and special donations. You may wish to advertise your cattery, kittens or stud service in the show book, and this will cost you so much for part of a page or a whole page. You also may want to contribute money toward special ribbons or trophies for special awards, such as Best Burmese Kitten, and any other award you wish to single out. You will receive a confirmation of your entry including directions on how to reach the location of the show hall and what motels nearby will allow your cat if you are planning to travel some distance and stay over.

PLANNING TO GO TO SHOW

Decide what you have to take to the show. The entry information will usually tell you that the show will supply a litter box and litter, plus food dishes and maybe even horsemeat. You will find there is certain equipment that you will need to bring along. You may find that a baby's overnight diaper bag will meet your needs, as it can be carried over the shoulders and spillables can be carried upright. You will need the following: curtains, towels, sheets or some draping to enclose the cage and separate your animal from his neighbor to keep him less excited and cut down on the risk of his contracting something at the show. Towels and sheets can be held in place with colorful plastic clothes pins. Or, you can get fancy and make drapes considering that the average cage is 25 inches square on each side. You can make them like regular curtains, and use curtain rods, holding them in place with pipe cleaners. Cat exhibitors are inventive and necessity, you will find, is the mother of invention.

In addition, you should find something soft for the bottom of the cage. A bathmat or small rug will do nicely. You can become decorative and use colors that enhance your cat's color. Remember that spectators will be viewing your cat for two days. Be proud of him and make his cage show him off to advantage. You should also bring with you your supplies to clean your cat up if he has an accident—in travel or while at the show. Naturally, you will have carriers to transport your cat or cats. You will need a suitcase for your drapes, curtain rods, rugs, etc. You will also need Q-tips or cotton balls to clean the eyes should they run before the cat is shown. If possible use a baby bottle or another unbreakable bottle and bring your own water so that water change won't affect your cat's bowel movements.

Bring dishes in case none are supplied. Dry food can be brought if you are not sure about show authorities' supplying food. It is not messy and is good for the two short days of the show. Show cleaner is a must in case your cat gets dirty or makes a mess. Paper towel is also necessary for cleanup operations. Pipe cleaners are helpful in securing curtain rods and they have other good uses.

Bring all papers necessary for the particular show and any necessary if you are selling kittens, including a receipt book for people paying outright or paying down-payments. Bring your entry confirmation, registration papers for the association, and pedigree. A pad and pen are also useful and don't forget grooming tools such as brushes, combs and cloths for a final touch-up before the cat goes into the judging ring. A week before the show either have your cat bathed or do it yourself. It will take a few days for the coat to reach its peak of beauty after a bath. Groom all week, get out those tangles, fluff up that ruff; on shorthairs smooth down that coat and make it shiny. Then, on the night before the show, get a good night's sleep. Remember to use the coat and skin conditioner faithfully a few weeks before the show to keep the cat's fur and coat at its best.

AT THE SHOW

When you reach the show hall bring in the cats only. You will probably find a line awaiting the vet. All cats must be checked by a vet before entering the hall. The vet will check for conditions that can be passed on to other cats at the show. They will check for declawing, which is not allowed for any cat competing in the championship classes. A good breeder will not bring a cat who has been sick within twenty-one days of the show or which comes from a cattery where sickness has been prevalent within the same time period. The vet usually is on duty between eight and ten in the morning.

After the cat is checked you will be assigned a cage, or you may be able to pick one yourself. If the latter is the case, and there are two of you attending the show, one

Miniature Siamese 2¾ lbs.
Miniature's name: The Katerwol Kalif, blue point male
Owner: Mr. and Mrs. Charles L. Schmidt
Photo: Leslie Buckingham

should stay with the cat or cats and the other should select a cage. You will get a number for each cat; that will be your cat's "name" for the entire show. Put the number on the cage and the card you get with the cat's name, yours and the cat's number.

If you need to do any transferring of your cat from one competition class to another or from one color class to another do it as you enter so the judges in the rings will have the information when they begin judging. Now, set up your cage. Put up the drapes, put in a rug, the box and litter, and water and food. Then when cage is ready, put the cat in. You may have brought your own food, coffee,

Danish, or sandwiches in a cooler. If not, you will probably be looking for some coffee and something to eat before the show opens. You will already have had a busy time. Now you can relax (comparatively) and read the show book. Here you will find your cat listed, who the judges are (this may have been listed in *Cats* Magazine or on the entry form information sheet), and also advertisements. There should also be a list of awards in each ring and a list of final awards for each ring. On a separate sheet and sometimes in the show book you will find a listing of the show schedule. This tells when the cats will come up for judging and in what rings. All cats of a breed come up together until they are all judged; then the next breed is done and so on. Each cat is judged in four rings, by four different judges. The show book will tell you what you most want to know and what your competition will be. Now, you can go and take a peek at the other cats. You can better enjoy the judging if you understand the book that is your directory for the show. Below is an example of a typical page.

	Neff	Neff	RI	
CLASS10MGC SHELL CAMEO	AB	SP	AB	SP
MALE GRAND CHAMPION				
100 Minuet FROSTED SUNSET of				
Mer-C 10MI-41561 8/23/67	——	——	——	——
Storm Dancer of Araho ex. Darker				
Clown Princess of Minuet Br:				
Mrs. Talley Ow: Dr. and Mrs.				
Eugene Couture				
CLASS10FN SHELL CAMEO				
FEMALE NOVICE				
101 Wicksford's POWDER PUFF of				
Theta 10FN-17563 6/9/69	——	——	——	——
Ginger Sinbad ex. Wickford's				
Sheba Br. George O'Neil				
Ow: Mr. and Mrs. Robert Wilson				

Now, to interpret. The class and color number is given and underlined, all in capital letters. Under that is the sex and competition class, also all in capitals. #100 is a male and a grand champion, #101 is a female and a novice. The cat's number at the show is given in the left margin (100 and 101), then the cat's name is given with the cattery it came from first (in small letters), the cat's name (in capital letters) and the cattery it now belongs to (in small letters). Take, for example, Minuet FROSTED SUNSET of Mer-C. The cat came from Minuet cattery, his name is Frosted Sunset and he now belongs to Mer-C cattery. Next the cat's registration number in the association is given and its exact birthday (those given here are fictitious). After that the sire and dam are given. Sire: father; Dam: mother. Br. indicates breeder of the animal. OW. indicates the owner. To the right you will notice the abbreviations Neff and RI and just below AB and SP. In this particular show the two former are abbreviations for the two cat clubs putting on the show (this is only the cat club, not the association supporting the cat club). Here the Neff stands for Northeast Feline Fanciers and RI stands for the Rhode Island Cat Club. The latter two abbreviations are to distinguish what type of ring it is. AB means that the ring is an all-breed ring, SP means that this is a speciality ring. This is important as in the all-breed rings, the finals include all the breeds judged, both longhair and shorthair. On the other hand, a speciality ring will judge the longhairs and then do finals including only longhairs. Then the same judge will do shorthairs and the finals for these cats. Obviously, in the speciality rings your cat is competing only against cats of his speciality be it longhair or shorthair. In order to get a championship at a show your cat must take a winner's ribbon in all four rings. (In one association you can win with three winner's ribbons out of four rings.) As you sit and view the judging you can mark your book, where the space is left, as to which cat got first, second, third, best of color, best of breed; and finally at the end of the day who got best of each major class: novice, open, champion, and grand champion as well as the cat of the opposite sex, who took opposite sex wins in all these classes.

Now that you know how to read a showbook you can walk around and see the other breeds, view the judging and wait for your cat to be called up for the big moment. With a kitten, chances are this will occur four times on the first day of the show. For a cat, you will probably be judged twice each day for a total of four rings by four different judges. When your number is called bring your cat up and place him in the cage under his number in the judging ring. Then sit down and wait. Do not disturb the judge, who will probably be going over previous judging and will try not to notice who owns which cat. Do not call attention to yourself or your cat. The judge should be unaware of whom the cat belongs to.

Your cat will be judged with others of its breed and color. Do not be afraid of how your cat will act. If he is used to kind treatment he will probably allow an experienced judge to handle him. The judges handle cats with authority and the cats sense it. You will, of course, have groomed him one final time before bringing him up and, hopefully, you will have provided enough human contact in your home or cattery so that your cat will not be fearful of being handled. The more a cat is handled and well, with authority, the better he will act in the show ring. Should your cat act up, the judge will probably ask for the cat's owner (you) to hold the animal while the judge looks the cat over. Judges will not count down a cat who behaves skittishly, but you may be a little embarrassed. Do not be, it can happen to any cat owner. As the judge looks at your cat he will be looking for the qualities described in Chapter 1. The question is: which cat of each color and breeds come best up to the standards, the description, given in the association's "standards." As stated, the descriptions of each breed (and their individual colors) in Chapter 1 include these standards in general as stated in most of the standards of the various associations. They vary little from association to association. Now, sit back and watch the judging and good luck.

JUDGING CLASSES

In this section of the book we will examine six examples of how cats are broken down into classes for judging at cat shows. The breakdown varies in different associations. The associations discussed are those best known across the country—those having the most shows. As stated before, it is wise to have a copy of each association's show rules and show standards. Know the association you are dealing with and don't depend on them being all alike. If they were, there would be no need for more than one association. First, let's look at the breeds and colors accepted by the different associations as of the last printing of their rules and standards (May 1970). All the breeds are in small capitals, the special divisions within a breed are in italics and the color classes within the breeds are in lower case.

CFA: Cat Fanciers' Association, Inc.
BALINESE: chocolate, seal, lilac and blue.
BIRMAN: (SACRED CAT OF BURMA) chocolate, seal, lilac, blue.
HIMALAYAN: chocolate, seal, lilac, blue, flame, tortie.
PERSIAN: *Solid Color Division:* white (blue eyed, copper eyed and odd-eyed), blue, black, red, red peke-faced, cream. *Shaded Division:* Silver (Chinchilla and shaded), shell cameo and shaded cameo. *Smoke Division:* black smoke, blue smoke, cameo smoke. *Tabby Division:* silver, red, red peke-face, brown, blue, cream, cameo tabby; silver, red, brown, blue, cream, cameo mackerel tabby. *Particolor Division:* Tortoiseshell, Calico, Blue-cream.
ABYSSINIAN: Ruddy, red.
AMERICAN SHORTHAIR: white (blue, copper and odd eyed), blue, black, red, cream, chinchilla silver, shaded silver, black smoke, blue smoke, silver, red, blue, cream tabby; silver, red,

blue, cream mackerel tabby; tortoiseshell, calico, blue-cream.

BURMESE

COLORPOINT SHORTHAIR: lynx point, red point, tortie point.

EXOTIC SHORTHAIR: White (blue, copper and odd eyed), blue, black, red, cream, chinchilla silver, shaded silver, shell cameo, shaded cameo, black smoke, blue smoke, cameo smoke, silver, red, brown, blue, cameo, cream tabby; silver, red, brown, blue, cameo, cream mackerel tabby; tortoiseshell, calico, blue-cream.

HAVANA BROWN

KORAT

MANX: White (blue, copper and odd eyed), blue, black, red, cream, chinchilla silver, shaded silver, black smoke, blue smoke, silver, brown, blue, cream tabby; silver, brown, blue, cream mackerel tabby; tortoiseshell, calico, blue cream, bicolor (red and white, blue and white, cream and white, or black and white).

OMC: white with smoke, any tabby pattern tortie or blue cream.

REX: white (blue, copper and odd eyed), blue, black, red, cream, chinchilla silver, shaded silver, black smoke, blue smoke, silver red, brown, blue, cream tabby; silver, red, brown, blue, cream mackerel tabby, tortoiseshell.

RUSSIAN BLUE

SIAMESE: chocolate, seal, lilac, blue.

PROVISIONAL BREED—ANGORA: blue eyed white, copper eyed white, odd eyed white.

NCFA: National Cat Fanciers Association, Inc.

ABYSSINIAN: ruddy, red.

BURMESE: seal brown, champagne, blue.

DOMESTIC SHORTHAIR: white (blue-copper-odd eyed), blue, black, red, cream, shaded silver, blue smoke, black smoke, blue, red, brown, silver tabby; blue, red, brown, silver mackerel tabby; tortoiseshell and white, tortoiseshell, particolor, cream tabby.

MANX: white (blue, copper and odd eyed), blue, black, red, cream, chinchilla, shaded silver, blue smoke, black smoke, blue, red, brown, silver tabby; blue, red, brown, silver mackerel tabby; tortoiseshell and white, blue cream, tortoiseshell, particolor.

PERSIANS: *Solid Color Division:* white (blue, copper, odd eyed), blue, black, red, peke faced red, cream. *Tabby and Tortie Division:* red, peke faced red, brown, silver tabby; tortoiseshell and white, blue cream tortoiseshell. *Himalayan Division:* frost, blue, chocolate, seal, red and tortie point. *Balinese Division:* frost, blue, chocolate, seal, red, tortie point. *Silver Division:* Chinchilla silver, shaded silver, blue smoke, black smoke. *Cameo Division:* shell cameo, shaded cameo, smoke cameo, cameo tabby.

RUSSIAN BLUE: solid blue.

KORAT: silver blue.

HAVANA BROWN

SIAMESE: frost, tortie, blue, chocolate, seal, red, albino point.

Already you can make comparisons between associations and understand why there are more than one association. Each does recognize some breeds that others do not. Some also recognize different colors within the breeds. They also do not put the same breeds and colors in the same classes or divisions. As you can see, the NCFA puts all longhairs together under PERSIANS, where the CFA recognizes the BALINESE and HIMALAYAN as a breed, not a color division. Also note the cameo division. Even in breaking down colors into divisions, there are differences: In CFA the shell cameo and shaded cameo come under the *Shaded Division,* the red or smoke cameo comes under the *Smoke Division,* and the cameo tabby comes under the *Tabby Division.* In NCFA they are all in the *Cameo Division.* This is important because this is the breakdown of breeds, colors, and divisions that the judges will award ribbons in. Again, buy a copy of the rules and standards so you will know what these differences are from association to association. Let's look at a few more well known associations and how they class breeds and breed colors.

CFF: Cat Fanciers' Federation, Inc.
PERSIAN, MANX, REX, AMERICAN DOMESTIC SHORTHAIR: *Solid Color Division:* white (blue, copper, odd eyed), black, blue, red, peke faced red, cream.
HAVANA BROWN
RUSSIAN BLUE
BURMESE: sable, blue, champagne.
ABYSSINIAN: ruddy, red.
Siamese Division: chocolate, seal, lilac and blue point.
Himalayan Division: Chocolate, blue, lilac, seal, flame, blue cream point and tortie point.
BALINESE: choclolate point, seal point, lilac point, blue point.
Shorthair Colorpoint Division: red.
Silver Division: chinchilla, shaded silver.
Smoke Division: blue, cameo and blue smokes.
Cameo Division: shell and shaded.
Tabby and Tortie Division: silver, cream, red, red peke face, brown, blue, cameo tabby; silver, cream, red, red peke face, brown, blue, cameo mackerel tabby; mackerel tabby manx and rex, tortoiseshell, tortoiseshell and white, calico, blue cream.

ACA: American Cat Association, Inc.
Solid Color Division: Persians, Domestic Shorthair, Manx, Maine Coon white (blue, copper and odd eyed), blue, black, red, red peke faced, cream.
KORAT
LAVENDER FOREIGN SHORTHAIR
ALBINO FOREIGN SHORTHAIR
HAVANA BROWN
BRITISH BLUE
RUSSIAN BLUE

BURMESE

Silver Division: Silver and shaded silver Persians, shaded silver domestic shorthairs.

Smoke Division: Black smoke Persians, Manx, Rex, Maine Coon and Domestic Shorthair. Blue smoke Persians, Rex, Manx, Maine Coon and Domestic Shairhair. *Tabby and Tortie Division:* for Persians, Maine Coon, Manx, Domestic Shorthair and Rex: cream, blue, silver, brown, red, red peke face tabby, blue, silver, brown, red, red peke face mackerel tabby, tortoiseshell, tortoiseshell and white, calico, blue cream. *Cameo Division:* shell, shaded, smoke and tabby for Persian, Domestic Shorthair, Manx, Rex. *Colorpoint Division:* Himalayans: lilac, blue, chocolate, seal and red point. Siamese: lilac, blue, chocolate, seal.

Colorpoint shorthairs: lilac, blue, chocolate, seal and red points; lilac, blue, chocolate, seal tortie points; lilac, blue, chocolate, seal lynx points.

BALINESE: lilac, blue, chocolate and seal points.

SACRED CAT OF BURMA: lilac, blue, chocolate, seal points.

ACFA: American Cat Fanciers Association

ABYSSINIAN: red, ruddy.

AMERICAN SHORTHAIR DOMESTIC: white (blue, copper and odd eyed), blue, black, red, cream, chinchilla silver, shaded silver, blue smoke, black smoke, blue, red, cream, brown, silver tabby; blue, red, cream, brown, silver mackerel tabby; blue cream, tortoiseshell and white, parti-color, tortoiseshell, any other color.

BALINESE: frost, blue, chocolate, seal and red point.

BRITISH BLUE

HAVANA BROWN

KORAT

COLOR POINT: lynx point.

BURMESE: seal brown.

HIMALAYAN: frost, blue, chocolate, seal, red, tortie point.

RUSSIAN BLUE

MAINE CAT: *Solid Color Division:* white (blue, orange, odd eyed), blue, black, red, cream. *Tabby and Tortie Division:* blue, red, brown, silver tabby; blue, red, brown, silver mackerel tabby; tortoiseshell and white, blue cream, tortoiseshell, cameo tortoiseshell. *Silver Division:* chinchilla silver, shaded silver, blue smoke, black smoke. *Particolor Division:* all variations. *Cameo Division:* shell cameo, shaded cameo, cameo smoke.

PERSIANS: same as Maine Coon Cat but add cameo tabby to Tabby and Tortie Division as of May 1, 1971 and add peke faced red tabby to same division. Also add red peke face to Solid Color Division.

MANX AND REX: same as American Domestic Shorthair.

A.O.C.: any other color.

SIAMESE: frost, blue, chocolate, seal, red.

UCF: United Cat Federation, Inc.

ABYSSINIAN: red and ruddy.

ALBINO FOREIGN SHORTHAIR

BURMESE: sable, champagne, blue and platinum.

COLORPOINT SHORTHAIR: red, seal, tortie, chocolate tortie, blue tortie and frost tortie point.

DOMESTIC SHORTHAIR: all colors of longhairs plus cream tabby.

EUROPEAN SHORTHAIR: all longhair colors.

HAVANA BROWN

KORAT

LAVENDER FOREIGN SHORTHAIR

MANX: all colors.

REX: all colors.

RUSSIAN BLUE

SIAMESE: seal, frost, blue, chocolate.

LONGHAIR: *Solid Color Division:* white (blue, odd and copper eyed), blue, black, red, red peke faced, cream. *Silver Division:* chinchilla, shaded. *Smoke Division:* blue, black. *Cameo Division:* shell, shaded, smoke, tabby. *Tabby Divi-*

sion: silver, red, red peked face, brown, blue. *Parti-color Division:* tortoiseshell, blue cream, calico. *Himalayan Division:* frost, blue, chocolate, seal, flame. *Balinese Division:* frost, blue, chocolate, seal.
In tabby both classic and mackerel patterns are accepted.

JUDGING AND AWARDS

As already stated and shown, each association places breeds and their colors into different competition classes and color divisions. For the most part, however, similar awards are given in all associations. In addition to these regular awards, people may donate special awards for special wins. Trophies are sometimes given, sometimes money (rarely though), sometimes ribbons and often subscriptions to *Cats* Magazine. In each ring the judging is the same as each breed comes up to be judged. The judge will pick the best male and best female of each color and breed, within the novice class first. These will receive a blue ribbon for a first award. Then for the same breed and color a second-, third-, and sometimes fourth-place ribbon will be given. Then the Open competitors will be judged in the same manner and awarded their ribbons. Then the judge will decide between the male winner of the first ribbon in the novice and in the open class and award the winner's ribbon for the point toward championship. He will then do the same with the female of the same breed and color. He will then go on and judge for the first award in the championship class for both female and male, each judged separately. Judging will then be done for the color award or Best of Color ribbon. The cat judged best of color of all the cats within that breed and color will receive a ribbon which reads Best of Color or Best of Class (meaning color class). Then he will check for the opposite sex color winner. If a male gets best of color, he will award the best female of the same color the BOX color ribbon (BOX meaning best opposite sex). If, in the particular judging, there are divisional awards to be made they will then be made or the judge may leave these awards for the finals.

The divisional awards usually mean a rosette (a fancy ribbon for the winner and winner of best opposite sex in the division). For example, suppose the judging is being done on Persians and the cameo division has been called up by number. Here will come shell cameos, shaded cameos, and smoke cameos (depending on how the association groups its colors). There will be both female and male cats. The judge will start with the shell cameos and look at the males first (as the order goes in the show book). He will choose the first, the best, male shell cameo novice. Then he will choose the first, the best, male shell cameo open. Then he will award the winner's ribbon by deciding which of these two who received first ribbons will get the winner's ribbon. Then he will do the same with the shell cameo novice female and shell cameo open female. After this he will decide which of all the shell cameos should get best of color. Should it be a male, he will look to the females for his BOX (best opposite sex) color ribbon. He will then go on and do the same procedure with all the other cats, first the shaded cameos and then the smoke cameos. When all have been done he will look for the divisional winners. Naturally, he will consider only those who have won the highest awards already. He will then award a best cameo and a BOX cameo rosette, to the best cameo and the best cameo of the opposite sex.

The following are what is officially known as the competitive classes:

NOVICE: All cats, male or female, eight months old or order who have never won a first place at a show put on by the particular association. These cats are usually under two years of age.

OPEN: For males and females, eight months old or over who have won a first place ribbon in the association or who have reached the age of two years.

CHAMPION: For males or females who have won their championship (but not double or senior championship, where possible) by winning four winner's ribbons under a designated number of judges. These cats must have obtained a confirmation of championship after becoming champions. They will compete together, male against male, female against female, for wins towards a double championship, triple or senior (in one association) and finally to a grand championship.

GRAND CHAMPION: These cats are confirmed grand champions having qualified according to the particular association's criteria. They will compete for double grand championship.

Other classes in the show include the spays and neuters, sometimes known as peerless or premiership class. They compete on the same basis as champions, but in separate competition. Once champions, they may be called champion peerless or premier depending on the association. A whole cat may later compete for wins in the altered class once altered. This cat will retain his previous title, and will start again as a novice in the altered division.

Another class that is judged is the kitten class. This is for males and females that are at least four months old and not older than seven months. They are judged by breed and color and given ribbons for first, second, third, and so on as designated. Then awards for best kitten, second-best kitten, best kitten opposite sex, and so on may be given.

The household pet class is a fun class, open to all cats who do not have pedigrees. They may be hybrids or may not meet the standards of the championship classes. They are judged for disposition and beauty, as well as condition.

The last class is the A.O.V. class where cats of a new breed or color are judged for best, best of color and best A.O.V.

Ribbons for shows usually bear the colors of the club

or association; but the first, second, third, and fourth and winners ribbons are usually the same. First is always blue, second is red, third is yellow, and fourth (if given) is green. The winner's ribbons are either red, white, and blue; or purple.

In addition to the awards already mentioned there are final awards given for each ring. There are kitten finals for the best kittens (as many bests as the association wants to award). In household the same awards are given as in the kitten class, as many bests as are designated by the association. In championship competition there are two finals including all the cats in the show. These are held in each of the all breed rings. The awards given usually are best novice, BOX novice, best open, BOX open, best champion, BOX champion, Best grand champion, BOX grand champion, second-best cat, best cat opposite sex and best cat. In the speciality rings the same awards are given, but they are given twice. In each of the two rings, the longhairs are given the above awards and then the shorthairs are given the same awards or vice versa. In the altered class the same awards may be given as in the regular championship class, or the association may give only second-best alter, best alter opposite sex, and best alter. Often there is an additional award given in the judging of each breed; that is, best of breed and best opposite sex of breed. For example, best Persian and BOX Persian.

For the smaller awards, ribbons and rossettes are given. For the final wins, trophies are usually given. We will examine each association (as again, each is different in the ways it awards its titles) to find out how you can make your cat a champion.

CFA: Within a breed and color the winning cat of each sex in the Open class will compete with the winning cat of its sex in the Novice class for winner's ribbon. Four winner's ribbons under three judges constitute a championship. This must be claimed with a dollar fee within 60 days.

ACA: four wins under three judges by a cat of a color class. Championship must be claimed in 60 days.

UCF: The first place novice competes with the first place open of the same sex and color for the winner's ribbon. Four winner's ribbons under four different judges gain a championship. Claims must be made in 60 days.

NCFA: The winning male of a breed and color in open competition competes with the winning male of a breed and color in the Novice competition for the winner's ribbon. Claims must be made.

CFF: Four winner's ribbons under at least three judges. Champions must make their claims in 60 days.

ACFA: Four winner's ribbons in the same color class under four judges and confirmation of championship.

For Grand championship the following must be won:

ACFA: A cat must be a quadruple champion after having become a double champion (in seven shows under six judges) and a triple champion (in ten shows under eight judges), then the cat must win champion winner's ribbons in three additional shows under three judges (shows are defined as showing in a judging ring). The cat must also have qualified for, and been issued, a certificate of royal merit, receive four final awards under four different judges in championship classes, one of such four final awards being best champion or BOX champion. Claim must be made of such an award.

In ACFA it is possible for your cat to earn what is known as Merit Awards. A Certificate of Merit may be won if your cat has scored not less than 85 points under not less than five judges. You will be given your cat's score after he is judged. A High Merit may be earned with 90 points under seven judges. A Royal Merit takes 95 points under seven judges.

CFA: The best champion receives one point for every champion present and defeated in the show. Best Premier received two points for each Premier present. Divisional points, best of any division, gives one point for every champion present and defeated. Best Opposite Sex champion and Best Champion longhair or shorthair gets one point for every cat of the speciality beaten. One hundred points are required for grand champion. They must be won under at least three different judges. At least one win must be best champion in any show or best shorthair or longhair in any show.

ACA: An accumulation of a minimum of 15 grand champion points in either all-breed or speciality shows under three judges. Male or female judged best champion or BOX champion gets one point for every four champions competing for best champion and one-half point for every other four for Box champion. Best of breed gives one point for every four champions of that breed present. Best cat in show gets two points. Second best cat gets 1½ points, best in show BOX gets one point. Best longhair or shorthair and not best champion gets one point for every four champions of the same speciality group.

CFF: Best shorthair or longhair gets one point for every four champions. If more than four the cat gets ¼ point for each additional champion. Best champion in show gets ¼ point for each champion competing. Best longhair or shorthair BOX gets ½ point if four champions are competing and ⅛ for every cat if over four are competing. Fifteen points won under at least three judges and one win as best champion or best champion opposite sex wins a grand champion.

NCFA: When a cat has been confirmed a quadruple champion then it must compete in the senior championship class. To qualify for grand champion the cat must take at least one best senior champion or two best opposite sex senior champion wins in shows.

UCF: Best champion gets five points and best champion opposite sex gets three points. Speciality show: best champion gets four points; best opposite sex gets two points. Four points given for second-best cat in show if not Best champion or BOX Champion. Best of breed of division gets half a point except best champion and best champion opposite sex or second best cat in show. Fifteen points awarded by three or more judges and at least two wins of any one of the following: best champion, best opposite sex champion or second best cat.

7

For Fun and Profit: A Summary

At first you will be playing the cat game for fun. The money may seem to go out to buy equipment, food, cats, and to register all your cats and your cattery. Be patient: the money will come in with your kittens. However, keep a separate account. Use this to cover your expenses for showing and supplies. If you make a profit, all well and good. If you break even with a small cattery be grateful and enjoy your cats, as they are payment in themselves. Be patient above all. It takes time to make a championship, a grand, raise a cat, have a litter. Love your cats; they will be your greatest reward. It is a wonderful field, full of wonderful and individualistic people. The show world will become an enormous club of friends you will enjoy seeing again and again. Competition will raise your spirits and keep you in the competition. Taking care of your kits will be like being a parent all over again. Even without a profit, there is no business like the cat business. Just ask a cat owner!

Glossary

AGENT: Person designated by the owner of the cat to exhibit the cat in the show.

A.O.V. Purebreds with registered parents, but no established or recognized class for competition, compete in this class.

ALL BREED JUDGE: A judge licensed to judge all breeds.

ALL BREED SHOW: A show where both longhair and shorthair cats are shown.

ASSOCIATION: An organized group which keeps records of purebred cats, catteries, litters, and which sponsors shows and supports its clubs.

BOX: Best opposite sex.

BREED: All those cats of the same physical type such as Persians, Siamese, Manx, etc.

BREEDER: The person who owned the dam at the time of breeding.

CAT: A cat eight months or older of either sex, spayed or neutered.

CATALOG: List of the cats exhibited by their owners in a sponsored cat show. Listed by breed and color.

CHAMPION: A cat who has won three or four winner's ribbons, depending on the association involved.

COLOR CLASS: The colors within a breed, such as the blue point Siamese. These compete for best of class or best of color class.

COMPETITIVE CATEGORIES: These include novice, open, champion, grand champion, peerless, altered champion, premiership, kitten, household, A.O.V.

DISQUALIFY: To remove from competition.

EXHIBITOR: Owner, lessee, or agent or breeder who shows the cat at the show.

FANCIER: Person who owns and exhibits cats in sanctioned shows.

GRAND CHAMPION: Cat who has won the necessary points to qualify as a grand champion.

HM: High Merit. A cat who gets 90 points under 7 judges in ACFA.

HOUSEHOLD PET: A hybrid, crossbreed, cat with unknown parentage that is not eligible for registration but may compete in this class.

KITTEN: Under eight months of age, eligible for showing at four months, either sex, spayed or neutered.

LISTED CAT: One not registered with the association at the time of the show.

MERIT AWARDS: 85 points under five judges in ACFA.

NEUTER: A castrated male.

NOVICE: Open to all cats who have not yet won a winner's ribbon at a show sponsored by the particular association.

OMC: Other Manx colors.

OPEN: All open to all cats who have not won their championship but have won at least one winner's ribbon in the association.

ORC: Other Rex colors.

OWNER: Person to whom the cat is registered.

PEERLESS OR PREMIERSHIP: Spayed or neutered competition class, which is equivalent to championship.

REGISTERED CAT: One registered with the association putting on the show or registered with one or more associations.

RESERVE WINNER: Cat awarded this is the second-best cat and gets the first ribbon if the first winner is disqualified.

RING: Where judges judge cats by their breed and color.

RM: Royal Merit 95 points under 7 judges in ACFA.

SENIOR CHAMPION: Double champion, not yet a grand champion.

SHOW: Where cats are exhibited and judged. Sponsored by an association.

SHOW MANAGER: Conducts the show and generally sees that it runs smoothly.

SHOW SECRETARY: Does all the recording for the show and is in charge of all records.

SPAY: Altered female.

SPECIALITY JUDGE: A judge licensed to judge speciality shows.

SPECIALITY SHOW: Where cats of either longhair or short-hair are judged.

WITHHOLD AWARDS: When an award is not given because of a technicality.

Suppliers

ALCO CARRYING CASES, INC.
601 West 26th Street
New York, New York 10001

ANIMAL SPECIALITIES
P.O. Box 531
Camden, New Jersey 08101

ANIMAL VET-PRODUCTS INC.
P.O. Box 1491
Springfield, Illinois 62705

BIO-INDUSTRIES
P.O. Box 176
Alamo, California 94507

CATS MAGAZINE
10 California Avenue
Pittsburgh, Pennsylvania 15202

COLLAPSIBLE WIRE PRODUCTS
P.O. Box 691-K
Butler, Wisconsin 53007

FELINE ENTERPRISES
P.O. Box 99394
Louisville, Kentucky 40299

HADDELEIGH HOUSE
86 Ridge Road
Yonkers, New York 10705

NEW CENTURY CAT PRODUCTS
P.O. Box 50365
Chicago, Illinois 60650

SPECIAL PRODUCTS CO.
Dept. S, Box 861
Proverse City, Michigan 49684
WEE HEATHER PRODUCTS CO.
9969 East Miloann St.
Temple City, California 91780

Index